THE TRAVAIL OF THE FIRSTBORN

DOES GOD HATE ALL THE FIRSTBORN?

PROF. MICHAEL T. ADENITIRE, FABI; PH. D.

Ordering Information:

Prime Seven Media
518 Landmann St.
Tomah City, WI 54660

Printed in the United States of America

INDEX

Presentation

Hello, dear reader!

Welcome to a transformative journey that delves deep into the lives of firstborns, those unique individuals who carry the weight of expectation and legacy. This book was conceived from a burning desire to unravel the intricate threads of spiritual battles faced by firstborns, both now and throughout biblical history. As the oldest child, this exploration feels deeply personal, and I hope it resonates with you in ways that uplift and empower. What does it mean to be a firstborn? How do we reconcile the rich heritage of responsibility with the yearning for individual purpose? By examining these questions, we embark on an enlightening path filled with hope and redemption through faith in Jesus Christ.

In putting this book together, I pored over scriptures and delved into the lives of many individuals – some past, some present – who embody the heart of what it means to live as a firstborn. The journey of writing became an exploration of community, identity, and God's promises, proving that you are never alone in your struggles. Each chapter delves into the themes of biblical teachings while highlighting the practical implications of those teachings in our everyday lives. Our first chapter kicks off with the undeniable pressures that firstborns face, highlighting their history and cultural significance, and I look forward to you delving into those layers.

As we peel back the layers, expect to encounter tales of triumph, dark nights of the soul, and illuminating moments of realization that prove you can authentically embrace your identity through faith. Our exploration of the Fall of Man will reveal how that significant event forever altered the landscape for firstborns, introducing struggles that are all too familiar in today's world. It's amazing how much relevance ancient stories have in our modern lives, don't you think? But this isn't just theory! Prepare for gripping testimonies from firstborns, individuals who have wrestled through fear, disappointment, and victory all as a part of their journey. You're going to find yourself cheering for them, crying with them, and ultimately drawing inspiration from their compelling narratives! This book aims to be a living dialogue, inviting you to consider your own story, your own challenges, and finding strength through community support.

With each section, we'll tackle generational curses that may lurk in the background of your story, those forces that want to keep you trapped in cycles of doubt and negativity. But fear not! By the time we reach our powerful conclusion, you'll feel equipped to break those chains and step boldly into your God-given role. Expect to emerge not just informed but transformed!

Let's lean into the discussions that matter. We'll confront who you are in Christ, navigate through your identity, and ultimately invite you to embrace a victorious mindset. Together, we'll remind ourselves that firstborns are not just burden bearers but also change-makers, specifically designed to forge paths and inspire others. So, are you ready to embark on this journey with me? I promise you that it will be worth your while!

By engaging deeply with the stories, asking provocative questions, and finding reflections on your own life within these pages, I hope this book becomes not only informative but a trusted companion in your journey of discovery. We are all in this together, no matter where we find ourselves. And know that redemption is always within reach when we walk in faith.

So, grab that comfy blanket, settle into your favorite reading nook, and let's dive into this conversation. Expect revelations, beautiful insights, and, above all, hope. Here's to the journey ahead!

With heartfelt anticipation,

In hope and joy,

Prof. Michael T. Adenitire, FBI; PH.D.

CHAPTER 1

THE WEIGHT OF THE FIRSTBORN

Cultural Significance of Firstborns

The cultural significance of firstborns has played a pivotal role in shaping social norms and familial structures across various societies throughout history. From ancient civilizations to modern-day families, the status of the firstborn has been intertwined with notions of leadership, responsibility, and value. As we explore the multifaceted dimensions of this significance, we observe that the weight of being a firstborn transcends mere birth order; it encompasses a rich tapestry of expectations, customs, and spiritual

implications that have evolved.

Throughout history, societies have attributed special roles and privileges to firstborn children. In many cultures, the firstborn son is seen as a natural leader and the designated heir, often receiving preferential treatment in matters of inheritance and familial responsibilities. This is evident in ancient Israelite society, where the firstborn son received a double portion of the inheritance, given their role as the head of the family. Such customs not only reinforced the importance of the firstborn but also erected a foundation of expectations that could weigh heavily on their shoulders.

In ancient Egypt, the significance of firstborns was underscored by a deep-rooted belief in the divine nature of their position. The firstborn male was not merely a child but was viewed as a vessel of hope for the family's future. This belief manifested in various cultural practices, such as the ritual of naming the firstborn, which was directly tied to the family's aspirations and social standing. The firstborn son was often called upon to fulfill the family's dreams and ambitions, creating a legacy that would transcend generations. The weight of this responsibility could lead to immense pressure, often contributing to conflict and rivalry among siblings.

In contrast, some cultures have celebrated firstborn daughters with distinct customs. For example, in certain African societies, the firstborn daughter holds a revered position, often serving as a caregiver and protector of younger siblings. The expectation for her to nurture and guide her family fosters a strong sense of responsibility and pride in her role. The cultural significance attributed to firstborn daughters illustrates the complexities of gender roles and the varied definitions of leadership within familial contexts. These dynamics highlight that while firstborns may face similar societal expectations, their experiences can differ dramatically based on cultural contexts. Modern society presents a paradox regarding the significance of firstborns. In some contemporary families, the strict adherence to traditional customs has loosened considerably.

While the firstborn may still feel the burden of expectations, shifting societal norms often challenge these roles. Instances of parents projecting their aspirations onto their firstborns persist, as they grapple with the need to provide guidance and support while fostering independence. This delicate balancing act creates a new set of challenges for firstborns as they navigate the contemporary landscape of familial and societal expectations.

The evolution of the cultural significance of firstborns invites us to consider how these historical customs impact contemporary firstborns in their personal and spiritual lives. Many firstborns find themselves in a position where they bear the weight of expectations from family, society, and even themselves. The pressure to achieve, lead, and contribute can lead to internal struggles, such as feelings of inadequacy or the perpetual pursuit of perfection. These themes echo the experiences of many firstborns today as they balance autonomy with the weight of being a trailblazer in their families.

In spiritual contexts, the significance of firstborns resonates with biblical narratives that emphasize their role in God's plan. The stories of firstborns in scripture, such as Abel, Isaac, and Jesus, not only highlight the blessings associated with this position but underscore the challenges they faced.

The firstborns in the Bible often found themselves at the center of familial strife and spiritual warfare, paralleling the struggles faced by modern firstborns. For many, the exploration of their biblical significance serves as a source of reflection and inspiration, affirming the notion that they are called to a greater purpose.Firstborns today are often encouraged to embrace their identities through a lens of grace and understanding. Recognizing the cultural and historical significance of their birth order provides valuable context for their journeys. By examining the expectations placed upon them, firstborns can engage in reflective practices that foster self- acceptance and empowerment. This is essential for their spiritual growth, as they learn to navigate the tension between societal expectations and their desires.

Furthermore, the anecdotal experiences of firstborns reveal the nuances tied to their roles within the family unit. For instance, consider a firstborn son who has grown accustomed to being the 'man of the house' from a young age. He bears the weight of caring for his younger siblings and upholding the family legacy. As he transitions into adulthood, he often struggles with the duality of pride in his responsibilities and the pervasive fear of failure. This psychological dynamic illustrates the internal conflict many firstborns endure as they seek validation and acceptance from both their families and them.

Real-life examples further underscore how cultural significance manifests in personal experiences. Take, for instance, the story of a firstborn daughter from a traditional family who feels pressured to excel academically and socially, often sacrificing her personal aspirations for the family's expectations. While she may outwardly embrace her role as a supportive sister and daughter, internally, she grapples with resentment and a longing for self-discovery. These narratives not only highlight the weight of being a firstborn but also call attention to the importance of open dialogue within families about these expectations.

Cultural norms surrounding firstborns continue to shape their identities in complex ways. In cultures that heavily promote achievement, firstborns may feel inclined to consistently outperform their siblings, perpetuating a cycle of perfectionism that can be detrimental to their mental health. Conversely, in cultures that prioritize communal values over individual success, firstborns may find solace in the support of their families, leading to a more collaborative approach to leadership and responsibility. The interplay of these cultural values and expectations raises crucial questions for modern firstborns about their identities and place in the world.

As firstborns reflect on their experiences, it is essential to engage in conversations that challenge outdated norms and foster healthier dynamics within families. The exploration of the cultural significance of firstborns encourages open dialogues about the weight of expectations and the pressures that can accompany these roles. By addressing these issues, families can create spaces for mutual understanding and support, allowing firstborns to thrive without the burden of unrealistic expectations.

Moreover, the legacy of firstborns transcends individual experiences, impacting the broader community. Firstborns often emerge as natural leaders within their circles, drawing from their historical roles to inspire and guide others. Their experiences can catalyze positive change in their families and communities, as they embody resilience and strength in the face of adversity. The intersection of their cultural significance and personal experiences serves as a foundation for their leadership, making them vital contributors to their communities.

The firstborn's role, whether in ancient or contemporary contexts, extends beyond individual families. It encapsulatesa broader narrative about identity, expectation, and responsibility. As societies evolve, the cultural significance of firstborns must adapt to create a more inclusive understanding of leadership and success that transcends traditional norms. Embracing the diversity of experiences among firstborns allows for a more holistic perspective that cultivates empathy and understanding across different cultures.

Finally, the journey of firstborns serves as a reminder for all individuals of the importance of recognizing and embracing our unique identities. Rather than being confined by expectations, firstborns can choose to redefine their roles on their terms, empowering themselves in the process. This act of reclaiming one's identity is fundamental not only for personal growth but also for fostering spiritual deepening, as individuals align their paths with their authentic selves.

By delving into the cultural significance of firstborns, we illuminate the complex relationship between tradition, expectation, and personal experience. Understanding the historical context of these customs enables firstborns to navigate their identities with purpose and intention, empowering them to break free from limiting beliefs and embrace the fullness of their potential. As we encourage firstborns to reflect on their experiences, we open the door to a deeper understanding of the weight of their roles, ultimately leading them to a place of empowerment and redemption in a world that often places undue burdens on their shoulders.

CHAPTER 2

PSYCHOLOGICAL PRESSURES

The pressure that firstborns often experience can feel overwhelming, a silent weight that presses down on their shoulders from an early age. As the eldest in their families, these individuals typically find themselves thrust into roles laden with expectations and responsibilities. The cultural reverence for firstborns, prevalent across many societies, often leads to the assumption that they will be natural leaders, the most responsible among siblings, and the ones who set the standard for what success looks like within their families. This implicit understanding of their role can bring a potent mix of pride and pressure that colors their entire upbringing, shaping their self-image and affecting their relationships with family and peers.

Psychological studies have revealed that firstborns often display traits such as perfectionism and a heightened desire for approval. It's not unusual for these individuals to feel that their worth is contingent upon their performance, whether that's in academic settings, athletic pursuits, or family dynamics. The pursuit of excellence can become a double-edged sword; while it drives firstborns to achieve remarkable things, it can also lead to crippling stress and anxiety when they inevitably fall short of their own or others' expectations. Consider the story of Sarah, a woman in her early thirties who has always been the overachiever in her family. From a young age, she excelled academically, consistently receiving accolades for her performance. Her parents, proud of their firstborn, often celebrated her successes in front of the family, reinforcing the idea that achievement equaled love and admiration. However, the more Sarah excelled, the more pressure she felt to maintain that standard. Each A on her report card became not just a personal triumph but a prerequisite for affection and acceptance from her parents.

As Sarah transitioned into adulthood, this pressure manifested itself in unexpected ways. Although she graduated summa cum laude from college, landed a prestigious job, and appeared to have it all together, internally, she was battling feelings of unworthiness and inadequacy. Each professional milestone was marred by the fear that she would never measure up to the ideal she had constructed in her mind, one that was undoubtedly influenced by her upbringing as a firstborn. She found herself in a cycle where every success seemed to raise the bar higher, and every minor setback was a reminder of her perceived shortcomings.

In the realm of psychology, the phenomenon Sarah experienced is quite common among firstborns. Perfectionism is a recurring trait wherein individuals set unrealistically high standards for themselves, often driven by the desire for parental approval. This historical pressure can instill a mindset of fear of failing, of disappointing others, and of not living up to the ideal self that they've cultivated. According to research conducted by Dr. Alfred Adler, the founder of individual psychology, firstborns tend to internalize a sense of duty and responsibility, which can lead to anxiety, depression, and an overpowering sense of responsibility for others—a phenomenon he referred to as "over-parenting."

Interestingly, the psychological landscape for firstborns is often complicated by their relationships with their siblings. The family dynamic frequently creates scenarios where firstborns find themselves in a protective, authoritative role. They might feel the need to act as a caretaker for younger siblings while simultaneously competing for their parents' attention and affection. This duality can create an inherent conflict between the desire to lead and the desire to be acknowledged for their own experiences and achievements. Take John, another firstborn, who grew up in a household with three younger siblings. In his early years, he took it upon himself to be the role model that his parents expected him to be. The pressure was palpable; he was expected not only to succeed in school but also to be empathetic and nurturing towards his siblings. While he embraced his role with pride, he also felt a profound isolation. During his teenage years, he found it difficult to express vulnerability or seek reassurance from his parents—after all, he was the one who was supposed to be strong and capable.

As John transitioned to college, this strong persona created barriers in his relationships. While he was often seen as the go-to person for advice and guidance, he rarely allowed anyone to see his struggles. This façade came at a cost; he often felt lonely and disconnected, as though the weight of his responsibilities distanced him from both his friends and his family. It wasn't until he sought therapy years later that he began to untangle the complexities of his identity and the psychological pressures associated with being a firstborn.

The emotional toll stemming from these expectations can extend beyond achievements and responsibility, impacting many aspects of firstborns' lives, from academic pressure to romantic relationships. A desire for approval can lead firstborns to mold themselves to fit the expectations of their partners, sacrificing their own needs and desires in the process. In relationships, the need to please others can create significant stress, leading to feelings of inadequacy when they cannot meet those perceived demands.

Consider the narrative of Emily, who, as a firstborn, found herself engaging in a pattern of self-neglect in her romantic relationships. Rooted in her upbringing where her parents frequently emphasized the importance of maintaining family harmony, she learned to prioritize others' feelings above her own. Initially, her caring nature won her partners' affection; however, over time, the imbalance became suffocating. Emily often ignored her aspirations to support her partner's goals, yet deep down, she felt a growing sense of resentment and loss of self.

The psychological pressures tied to their roles often leave firstborns grappling with identity issues as they traverse adulthood. They might not always be able to discern whether their decisions are genuinely reflective of their desires or are simply the byproducts of ingrained expectations. In a quest to please, they may inadvertently forfeit their happiness and mental well-being.

This conundrum is underpinned by a profound struggle for self-definition, which calls for reflection and awareness. Firstborns must often engage in an internal dialogue that questions their motivations, fears, and aspirations—a journey toward self-acceptance and reclaiming their identities independent from external pressures. This journey can be sustained through various means, such as therapy, peer support groups, and faith-based communities. Building connections with others who have shared similar experiences often bears the fruit of trust and acceptance, allowing firstborns to explore their vulnerabilities in a safe environment.

Importantly, while the pressures of being a firstborn can lead to internal conflict, they can also foster resilience, empathy, and leadership skills that serve these individuals well throughout their lives. The manifestation of perfectionism can evolve into a healthy pursuit of excellence, and the burden of responsibility can transform into a passion for helping others succeed. Those who navigate these internal struggles often learn to harness their experiences and emerge with a renewed sense of purpose.

In examining the narratives of Sarah, John, and Emily, it becomes clear that firstborns are not alone in their struggles; they share common threads that weave through the tapestry of their experiences. Recognizing these psychological pressures is not only crucial in understanding their journeys but also essential in fostering empathy among peers, family members, and society at large.

Ultimately, the journey for firstborns involves navigating their roles while finding ways to express their authentic selves. By acknowledging their struggles, celebrating their achievements, and allowing space for healing, firstborns can transcend the pressures that seek to define them and carve out their own narratives. In doing so, they not only honor their unique identities as firstborns but also contribute to a broader conversation about the impact of familial dynamics and societal expectations on individual well-being. As we reflect on these stories and recognize the inner challenges faced by firstborns, we cultivate an environment where their victories are celebrated and their vulnerabilities are validated. By fostering a deeper understanding of their psychological landscapes, we empower firstborns to embrace their journey, navigate their challenges with grace, and emerge as resilient individuals ready to make their mark on the world.

Indeed, the path of the firstborn, while fraught with pressure, is also rich with potential testament to the strength that comes from overcoming not only the weight of their responsibilities, but the intricate tapestry of expectations woven into their lives.

CHAPTER 3

SPIRITUAL IMPLICATIONS

Being the firstborn carries a profound spiritual significance that echoes throughout biblical history and continues to shape the faith journeys of contemporary firstborns. From the beginning of scripture, we see the weight of identity, expectation, and the often-turbulent path that firstborns must navigate as they strive to fulfill their divine purpose. The stories of Cain and Abel, Isaac and Ishmael, and Passover illustrate the multifaceted roles that firstborns play, representing both blessing and challenge. Through these narratives, we can glean insights into the spiritual implications of being a firstborn and understand how these enduring themes can resonate with our lives today.

The story of Cain and Abel serves as a foundational narrative that highlights the complexities of being a firstborn. Cain, as the firstborn son of Adam and Eve, was given a prominent role in his family line, embodying both pride of place and heavy expectations. Scripture recounts how both brothers brought offerings to God, but it was Abel's offering that was accepted while Cain's was rejected. The weight of Cain's response reveals the inner turmoil that can accompany the identity of being a firstborn—feelings of jealousy and inadequacy. Rather than seeking to comprehend God's intentions, Cain allowed anger to fester, leading him down a path of betrayal and violence.

This story serves as a cautionary tale for firstborns today, illustrating how the pressures associated with their status can manifest destructive emotions if left unchecked. Many firstborns can relate to the instinctual drive to excel, often burdened by the unspoken expectations of their families and communities. Instead of competing with their siblings or striving for God's approval through comparison, firstborns should be encouraged to cultivate a relationship with God that turns their focus inward, to understand their unique gifts and identity as beloved children of God.

As we examine Isaac and Ishmael, we encounter the complexities of favoritism and the divergent paths that arise from the burdens tied to being a firstborn. Isaac, the legitimate son born to Abraham and Sarah, symbolizes God's fulfillment of promises. However, the narrative introduces Ishmael, Abraham's firstborn son, born of Hagar. This distinction complicates the notion of blessing linked to the firstborn, as both brothers faced unique challenges rooted in their lineage and circumstances.

The tension between Isaac and Ishmael illustrates that birth order does not automatically guarantee favor or impart divine purpose. This can resonate deeply for contemporary firstborns who may struggle with the weight of comparison, whether against siblings or expectations placed upon them by their families. The truth that emerges is that one's worth in God's eyes is not predicated on birth order, but on faith, obedience, and spiritual surrender.

Similarly, the story of the Passover further solidifies the spiritual implications of firstborns within the biblical narrative. During the Exodus, the firstborns of Egypt faced dire consequences, while the firstborns of the Israelites were marked by the blood of the lamb and spared from death. This act of redemption not only highlights the significance of the firstborns in the context of God's covenant with His people but also foreshadows the ultimate sacrifice made by Jesus Christ, the Firstborn of all creation.

Through the lens of the Passover, firstborns today can find a sense of hope and promise. Just as the Israelites were saved through the blood of the lamb, firstborns can embrace their identity in Christ as they accept His sacrifice. This new life invites firstborns to confront their fears and insecurities, fostering a transformative relationship with God that leads to personal freedom, and when they engage their faith authentically, they will begin to identify their own calling and purpose within the larger community of believers.

CHAPTER 4

THE FALL AND ITS CONSEQUENCES

Theological Foundations of the Fall

The Fall of Man represents one of the most pivotal events in the theological narrative, a moment that altered the trajectory of humanity and introduced profound consequences, both immediate and far-reaching. When Adam and Eve chose disobedience in the Garden of Eden, they opened the floodgates to sin, suffering, and spiritual warfare. This subchapter aims to explore the theological implications of the Fall while delving into its specific effects on firstborns, who often find themselves in a unique and difficult position within familial and spiritual contexts.

The narrative of the Fall is found in Genesis chapters 2 and 3, where the first humans are placed in a paradise with the simple command to avoid one tree—the Tree of the Knowledge of Good and Evil. The dimensions of this command establish the fundamental tenets of free will and obedience. Adam and Eve's decision to transgress God's command ignited a sequence of events that resulted in their expulsion from the Garden and the inevitable introduction of sin into human experience. The severity of their choice not only brought personal consequences but also seeded a cosmic struggle that continues to unfold.

The fact that the Fall is primarily attributed to the actions of Adam and Eve poses significant implications for firstborns. Traditionally, firstborns carry expectations for leadership and responsibility. They often serve as the family's representatives, shouldering burdens that younger siblings may avoid. This narrative structure can place a disproportionate weight on firstborns in the wake of the Fall. As seen in scripture, this weight may manifest as spiritual challenges and family dynamics marked by dysfunction.

As Adam and Eve faced their consequences—a disrupted relationship with God, a fractured bond with each other, and the emergence of a world marked by pain and toil—their actions reverberated through generations. According to Romans 5:12, "Therefore, just as sin came into the world through one man, and death through sin, and so death spread to all men because all sinned." This passage encapsulates the enormity of the Fall's effects. Sin became an inherited trait, passed down through humanity, affecting all people, including those born as firstborns.

Firstborns often feel the brunt of this inheritance. They encounter familial challenges born from the turmoil of the Fall, such as favoritism, competition, and conflict, famously illustrated in the stories of biblical figures like Cain and Abel. Cain, the firstborn son of Adam and Eve, succumbed to jealousy, leading him to commit the first murder in history. This biblical account showcases how sin's entry into the world distorts relationships and exacerbates strife, particularly affecting those in esteemed roles—the firstborns.

Theological reflection on the choices made by Adam and Eve helps us understand that the repercussions of the Fall extend far beyond individual guilt; they encompass the existential struggles of humanity. Sin not only disrupts our relationship with God but also sows discord within families. Firstborns are often placed in roles that require them to mediate familial tensions or aspire to fulfill lofty expectations imposed upon them. This dynamic can lead to significant emotional and spiritual burdens, resulting in anxiety, perfectionism, and feelings of inadequacy.

The duality of being a firstborn—a position that traditionally comes with admiration and responsibility—paired with the legacy of the Fall can create immense psychological pressure. Firstborns may feel compelled to succeed or take charge in ways that younger siblings do not. In light of spiritual warfare, this pressure can become a battleground where firstborns confront feelings of inadequacy and fear, battling against an enemy that seeks to exploit their vulnerabilities.

Ephesians 6:12 reminds us that our struggles are not against flesh and blood but against spiritual forces in the heavenly realms. This understanding of spiritual warfare is crucial for firstborns navigating their experiences in a fallen world. They are often prime targets for the cunning tactics of the enemy, who seeks to undermine their confidence and derail their potentials. The scriptures offer insight into how to combat these spiritual attacks, but it requires a deep understanding of both the theological underpinnings of the Fall and the inherent value of one's identity in Christ.

In grappling with the theological aspects of the Fall, it is essential to reflect on how these events resonate on a personal level for firstborns today. For example, when facing overwhelming familial pressure, firstborns can benefit from acknowledging that the responsibility they carry is part of the fallen condition rather than a true reflection of their worth or capability. It is vital for them to grasp that their identity and purpose rest in the redemptive work of Jesus Christ, the ultimate firstborn who overcame the consequences of the Fall. Jesus Christ is often referred to as the "Firstborn of all creation" (Colossians 1:15), symbolizing not only His preeminence but also His dual role as both creator and reconciler. He embodies the hope of redemption, offering firstborns the chance to reclaim their identities from the grips of familial expectations and spiritual oppression. Through Christ's sacrifice, firstborns can experience restoration that transcends the turmoil established by the Fall. This restoration teaches firstborns that their inherent value comes from who they are in God, not from the burdens placed on them by sin-laden family dynamics.

In embracing their identities as children of God, firstborns can draw strength from knowing that they are loved unconditionally and called to live out their lives in victory. Firstborns are positioned uniquely; they can break cycles of strife and lead their families towards healing.

But this mandate only comes through acknowledging the power of the Fall and overcoming its consequences through faith. By standing firm in faith and seeking God's guidance, firstborns can navigate their spiritual battles with resilience.

The story of redemption is a powerful testament to how God intends to transform the devastation of the Fall into something profoundly beautiful. Firstborns are invited to participate in this transformation, not only as recipients of God's grace but also as agents of change within their families and communities. As they reflect on their struggles in the light of God's truth, they can begin to reshape their narratives, focusing on their divine purpose rather than the weight of earthly expectations.

Additionally, it can be beneficial for firstborns to engage in spiritual communities that offer support and encouragement. Understanding that they are not alone in their struggles can help alleviate the burdens that often accompany their firstborn status. The church, as a collective body of Christ, can serve as a sanctuary where firstborns can find solace and strength as they confront the realities of their lives post-Fall.

As we explore the impact of the Fall through a theological lens, it becomes clear that understanding the roots of familial strife and spiritual warfare provides firstborns with invaluable insight. They are not merely victims of circumstance but rather participants in a larger narrative of redemption and restoration. Embracing faith and community can empower firstborns to rise above generational curses and familial expectations, establishing a new legacy grounded in love, faith, and hope.

In conclusion, the theological foundations of the Fall extend far beyond a simplistic understanding of sin and disobedience. The Fall introduced not only personal consequences for Adam and Eve but also a spiritual warfare that continues to impact humanity today—especially firstborns. By delving into the complexities of this theological narrative, firstborns can confront the challenges they face with a renewed sense of purpose and empowerment. Through Christ, they hold the keys to break free from the generational patterns established by the Fall, embarking on a journey of identity restoration and divine purpose. Embracing their role as firstborns— both within their families and in the larger context of the faith community— firstborns can claim their victory and live out lives that reflect the hope of redemption and the transformative power of God's love.

CHAPTER 5

CONSEQUENCES ON FAMILY DYNAMICS

The Fall of Man introduced a seismic shift not only to humanity's spiritual status but also to the intricate fabric of familial relationships. When Adam and Eve chose to disobey God, the harmony of their existence was fractured, giving way to a host of consequences that rippled through generations. One poignant area affected by this upheaval is the family dynamic, where rivalry, jealousy, and conflict often take root, particularly impacting firstborns who bear the weight of expectations and responsibilities.

Within families, the birth order often establishes a hierarchy, and firstborns frequently find themselves at the center of attention—deserving or undeserving. They are often seen as the pace-setters, the role models, and sometimes, the sacrificial lambs for the family's aspirations. Yet, this role does not come without its trials. The introduction of sin has tainted the sanctity of this position with jealousy among siblings, leading to misunderstandings that can result in irrevocable rifts.

To illustrate this, we can look to the biblical narrative of Cain and Abel. These two brothers, born into a world marred by sin, present a stark depiction of familial breakdown. Cain, the firstborn, wrestles with the weight of his status—the expectation to offer pleasing sacrifices and be a successful steward of God's creation. Abel, the younger brother, thrives in the favorable light of divine approval, powerfully emphasizing the theme of rivalry that emerges from comparative expectations. Cain's envy bubbles over, culminating in the tragic murder of his brother, a heartbreaking act that forever alters their family dynamics.

This story serves as a microcosm of the greater struggle faced by firstborns in any age. The pressures to achieve and satisfy family expectations often become suffocating, while the perception of favoritism or success of younger siblings can lead to deep-seated resentment. In modern examples, we can find similar themes playing out in our own lives, where the fruit of sin manifests as personal turmoil.

Consider the testimony of a woman named Sarah, the eldest of three siblings. She recalls how her parents always encouraged her to excel academically, pushing her toward achievements that they could boast about. The weight of their expectations began to feel like a straitjacket, leaving her little room to explore her own identity. When her younger brother, Jake, started to garner praise for his artistic talent, the atmosphere in the household shifted. Jealousy crept into their relationships, causing Sarah to feel that she was no longer the star of the family. Instead of celebrating Jake's successes, she found herself bitter and resentful.

In instances like Sarah's, it's evident that the Fall has consequences that echo through generations. As firstborns internalize these pressures, the emotional turmoil can manifest not only in familial relationships but also in their personal lives, leading to stress, anxiety, and diminished self-worth. The expectations placed upon them often feel unrelenting, drowning out their need for affirmation and acceptance.

The rivalry becomes a battleground not just for approval from parents, but also for love and recognition from the entire family unit. The harsh reality is that firstborns often find themselves pitted against their siblings, unable to appreciate each other's gifts due to the blinding haze of envy. The very essence of connection—love, support, and trust—becomes fragile when plagued by sin.

Through the lens of another familial story, we see the effects of expectation and rivalry intertwined. The Martinez family consists of three daughters, with Elena being the eldest. Known for her academic prowess, Elena was always praised for bringing home straight A's. With such high expectations resting heavily on her shoulders, she felt the pressure multiply when her middle sister, Mari, began to showcase her athletic talents. Suddenly, Elena was caught in a tug-of-war between her own achievements and the praise that Mari now received. The family's conversations shifted, spotlighting Mari's athleticism and accomplishments, while Elena felt her own identity was fading into the background.

As the rivalry deepened, so too did the misunderstandings. One evening at dinner, a casual comment about the upcoming sports competition ignited a fierce argument. Elena perceived her father's pride in Mari's accomplishments as betrayal, igniting feelings of inadequacy and hurt. Mari, on the other hand, could not understand why her sister was unable to celebrate her success, interpreting her silence as disdain.

In both narratives, we witness how sin has disturbed familial peace, leading to strife and disconnection. The fall's consequences become painfully evident when loved ones cannot provide each other with the support they need, instead viewing one another through the lens of competition. Times of celebration become tainted by unspoken feelings, and the once joyous experience of family gatherings transforms into a triggering minefield of insecurity and rivalry.

Furthermore, firstborns often bear the burden of mediating conflicts among their siblings or taking on the role of the peacemaker in the family. This assumed responsibility can further complicate their emotional journey. They may feel trapped in their roles, become resentful of the weight they carry, and struggle with their own desires and aspirations. As they navigate family dynamics, firstborns must grapple with their siblings' expectations and affections, leading to an inherent sense of conflict and potential discord.

Consider the Roberts family, who have a plethora of experiences that highlight this struggle. Alex the firstborn, mentors his younger siblings, providing guidance and support while secretly questioning his own abilities. He shares that many moments of family gatherings feel burdened by his role as the peacemaker, often sacrificing his own desires for harmony. When conflict arises, Alex internally wrestles with feelings of disappointment and frustration, and at times, finds himself longing for validation, the very thing he strives to provide to others.

The emotional turmoil experienced by firstborns serves as a reminder of the insidious nature of sin in familial relationships. Echoing throughout their experiences are feelings of inadequacy, a sense of rivalry, and a need for approval. The roots of these challenges lie not only in personal dynamics but also within a broader societal context. The narratives woven throughout Scripture, particularly those concerning firstborns, serve to illuminate and affirm these truths.

In addition to biblical narratives, the stories of modern families further explore the consequences of the Fall on family structure. One particularly poignant account comes from the Clarke family, where Peter, the oldest son, felt immense pressure to uphold his family's legacy in their family business. The expectations placed upon him created a vast chasm in his relationship with his younger brother, David, who felt overshadowed by Peter's accomplishments.

Peter's drive for success morphed into a relentless pursuit of perfection, consumed by the need to exceed expectations. David, feeling the burden of being compared to his older brother, eventually fell into a path of rebellion, distancing himself from the family business entirely. The rift became palpable when David decided to pursue a career in art—a field entirely different from the family's legacy. The brothers, once companions in childhood, became estranged by the very dynamics that were intended to bond them.

The emotional fallout from this struggle can be devastating. Peter, once fiercely competitive, now faced profound regrets about the lost relationship with his brother. As years passed with silence between them, the wounds festered, illustrating the deep consequences of familial rivalry rooted in sin.

Reflecting on such stories invites a moment of meditation on our family dynamics. Can we relate to the experiences of Sarah, Elena, Alex, Peter, or David? Each individual serves as a mirror through which we can examine our ties within our families. Are we fostering love and acceptance, or do we allow envy and rivalry to shape our relationships?

Encouragingly, while the narratives reflect the innate struggle firstborns face among siblings, they also offer space for healing and redemption. The important work of turning to God as a source of identity and affirmation can have transformative impacts on our family dynamics. Recognizing the power of grace can dissolve the toxicity often burdening our relationships.

As we contemplate the consequences of the Fall on family dynamics, we should seek out moments of reflection. Perhaps we need to initiate conversations with our siblings, share our struggles, and seek opportunities to celebrate each other rather than compete. Healing begins when we take a step of faith—carrying our burdens to God and leaning into the support of one another.

Additional opportunities for healing involve engaging in activities that foster connection rather than rivalry within our families. Pursuing shared interests can strengthen familial bonds, and creating traditions that celebrate each member's uniqueness can reshape the narrative. A family that embraces diversity of talents and passions can embark on a journey of discovery and unity, overcoming the toxic patterns of rivalry that often plague family life.

Furthermore, prayer becomes an essential component in navigating familial dynamics—inviting God into the often fraught relationships. Acknowledging one's struggles and asking for healing not only opens the door for divine intervention but also causes individuals to recognize their own shortcomings within relational barriers.

The Fall rendered humanity flawed, but through Christ's redemptive work, we are offered a new path—one that brings reconciliation, understanding, and restoration to our relationships. It's critical for firstborns to internalize their identity in Christ, a truth that provides comfort, acceptance, and purpose.

Through an honest exploration of the effects of the Fall on familial relationships, we begin to understand the complex nature of our interactions within family structures. The stories illuminate the challenges firstborns must navigate while simultaneously offering a reminder of hope and redemption through our relationship with Christ.

As we journey through life, may we always seek understanding, empathy, and grace in our familial dynamics—breaking the cycles of sin that lead to rivalry and division. In doing so, we prepare a pathway toward nurturing the bonds that ultimately reflect the heart of God's love and intent for our families. In recognizing and addressing the turmoil rooted in sin, we can work toward restoring harmony within the relationships that mean the most. May our stories intertwine with God's narrative of love, healing, and wholeness for future generations to come.

CHAPTER 6

SPIRITUAL WARFARE AGAINST FIRSTBORNS

In the grand tapestry of existence, the role of firstborns resonates with profound significance across family and societal landscapes. From the dawn of creation, firstborns have been seen as vessels of responsibility, expectation, and potential, often bearing a weight that transcends their mere biological status. However, as the narrative of the Fall illustrates, these roles have not only conferred honor and blessing but have also made firstborns prime targets in the ongoing battle between the forces of good and evil.

Spiritual warfare is a reality for all believers, but it seems that firstborns bear a unique brunt of these attacks. The Bible presents several instances that exemplify how the enemy focuses his efforts on undermining the identities and purposes of firstborns. The firstborn child in biblical history carries both a promise of inheritance and a potential for conflict. This duality lies at the heart of the spiritual struggles firstborns often face, as they embody not only the familial legacy but also the spiritual lineage established by God.

The theological foundation of the Fall introduces sin and its consequential separation from God, leading to an environment rife with conflict and strife. Firstborns, positioned within the family structure, often find themselves embroiled in the spiritual battleground that results from this separation. As the enemy seeks to exploit the vulnerabilities that arise from their roles, firstborns can experience spiritual attacks that manifest in feelings of inadequacy, fear, anxiety, and the overwhelming burden of expectations.

Take, for example, the account of Cain and Abel. Both brothers represented different aspects of familial dynamics, yet Cain, as the firstborn, succumbed to jealousy and anger, ultimately leading to the first murder. This chilling narrative highlights how the enemy can plant seeds of discord, particularly within sibling relationships, exploiting the firstborn's desire for acceptance and affirmation. Cain's actions testify to a broader spiritual reality in which firstborns must navigate the treacherous waters of rivalry and familial strife, a toxic landscape that can lead them far from their divine destiny.

Similarly, look at the life of Joseph, another biblical firstborn who faced severe adversity. Through betrayal by his brothers, enslavement, and imprisonment, Joseph's journey serves as a stark illustration of the spiritual warfare waged against firstborns. Yet, what makes Joseph's story powerful is not merely the suffering he endured but the divine purpose revealed through it. Each challenge was a tool used by God, ultimately leading Joseph to a position of prominence, where he could preserve many lives during a time of famine. His ability to remain faithful amid dire circumstances emphasizes the resilience intrinsic to firstborns, encouraging them to seek and embrace their God-given identity despite external pressures.

This narrative underpins the truth that while firstborns may be targeted for spiritual attack, they are also chosen vessels meant to carry the weight of God's blessing and redemption. They are forced into a battle not of their own choosing yet equipped with divine armor if they choose to take it up. Ephesians 6:10-13 reminds us that we "do not wrestle against flesh and blood, but against principalities, against powers, against the rulers of the darkness of this age, against spiritual hosts of wickedness in the heavenly places."

Understanding their positioning as firstborns, individuals must recognize that their inherent worth and purpose come from God. It is vital they stand firm against the enemy's schemes, realizing that the struggles they face are part of their calling to spiritual warfare. Firstborns are not merely meant to shoulder burdens but to rise as instruments of God's glory, reclaiming their identities through faith in Christ.

The sense of inadequacy can be one of the most debilitating feelings that firstborns encounter. They often carry the weight of parental expectations or the unfulfilled dreams of their predecessors. This familial pressure contrasts starkly with their inherent value as children of God. Just as God called to Moses from the burning bush, asking him to lead His people from bondage, firstborns too must respond to God's call, trusting in His provision and strength rather than succumbing to self-doubt.

Scripture speaks to these feelings of inadequacy. In Romans 8:31, Paul emphasizes that "if God is for us, who can be against us?" Firstborns must recognize that their worth is not measured by their ability to achieve or meet expectations but by their standing in Christ. Embracing their status as heirs to God's promises, firstborns can counteract feelings of insufficient worth by growing in their relationship with Jesus and understanding the truth of their identity. Fear is another weapon that the enemy uses adeptly. When the pressures of life mount, firstborns may find themselves ensnared in fear of failure, insecurity about their place in the family, and anxiety over fulfilling their responsibilities. This fear can lead to paralysis, hindering their progress and spiritual growth.

Isaiah 41:10 is a profound reminder to the anxious heart: "Fear not, for I am with you; be not dismayed, for I am your God; I will strengthen you, I will help you, I will uphold you with my righteous right hand." This affirmation transcends circumstances and speaks directly to the insecurities often felt by firstborns. The truth that God is present and actively working in their lives can shatter the stronghold of fear, offering a renewed sense of hope and courage to face whatever challenges may arise.

Anxiety, too, creeps in as part of the spiritual warfare targeting firstborns. The constant vigilance that comes with leadership—whether in the family or community—can breed anxiety when one is unsure of how to effectively lead or support those around them. The weight of responsibility can be overwhelming, leading to a cycle of worry that becomes spiritually debilitating.

Philippians 4:6-7 offers insight and a community remedy to anxiety, urging believers to present their requests to God "with thanksgiving." The promise that follows is that God's peace will guard their hearts and minds in Christ Jesus. Firstborns possess a unique opportunity to model reliance on God and prayer for those around them, all while battling their own struggles with anxiety.

As the challenges multiply, firstborns must recognize these feelings of inadequacy, fear, and anxiety as manifestations of the enemy's attacks in a larger cosmic struggle. These vulnerabilities are not merely personal struggles but signs of a spiritual confrontation where the enemy seeks to divert them from their identity in Christ. Understanding this dynamic helps to empower firstborns, encouraging them to take proactive steps toward spiritual victory. Engaging in spiritual warfare requires intentionality. Firstborns can employ various strategies to navigate these battles effectively. Developing a strong prayer life is paramount. Prayer gives voice to their struggles and invites divine intervention. Engaging in fervent prayer not only aligns them with God's will but also compels them to seek His wisdom and clarity amid turmoil.

Moreover, surrounding themselves with a supportive community can fortify firstborns against attacks. Fellowship within a church or close group of friends provides both accountability and encouragement. Sharing their burdens with trusted individuals can dismantle feelings of isolation, reminding them that their struggles are not theirs alone. Meditating on scripture is another vital component of spiritual warfare. The Word of God serves as both a sword and a shield against the lies of the enemy. By internalizing scripture, firstborns can draw strength from God's promises and counteract the negative thoughts that arise. For example, quoting verses that affirm their identity in Christ or remind them of God's faithfulness can shift their mental focus away from fear and toward faith.

Moreover, engaging in acts of service and outreach can help firstborns reclaim their identities in positive ways. By promoting love and hope within their circles, they shift the narrative from self-focused battles to those that embody the spirit of Christ. Serving others reminds them of their purpose, offering healing and perspective in the midst of spiritual warfare.

Ultimately, spiritual warfare is not merely a confrontation with external forces; it is a continual engagement in the battle for identity and destiny. Firstborns can lean into their role within God's family, recognizing that their lineage extends beyond earthly relatives into the rich tapestry of divine inheritance and purpose crafted by a loving Father.

The narrative of spiritual warfare is profoundly rooted in the understanding of the continuous struggle between light and darkness. Each firstborn is a vital part of this unfolding story, meant to arise amid contention as champions of faith. They must cultivate a firm foundation grounded in prayer, scripture, and community, recognizing they have been equipped with divine authority to overcome the challenges they face.

As we conclude this exploration of spiritual warfare against firstborns, it is essential to remember that these challenges signify part of a larger cosmic struggle. The plight of firstborns extends beyond individual experiences and speaks to the collective battle for identity, purpose, and legacy. In their fight against inadequacy, fear, and anxiety, firstborns are called not only to endure but also to thrive. They are invited into the redemptive work of Jesus Christ—transforming their struggles into stories of victory.

In the face of adversity, firstborns can find hope in the reminder that Christ, as the ultimate firstborn, faced the severest of trials, yet emerged victorious. By embracing His promises and seeking divine protection, they can walk boldly into their identities, reclaiming their purpose, and impacting the world around them. This, indeed, is the life of a firstborn set free, navigating the battles with the assurance that victory has already been secured through Christ.

CHAPTER 7

SATAN'S STRATEGY: THE TARGET ON FIRSTBORNS

Identifying the Enemy's Tactics

Throughout history, firstborns have been the subject of great expectations, unique responsibilities, and—most significantly—spiritual attacks. The enemy, Satan, has long recognized the intrinsic value of those who hold the title of "firstborn," whether through biological lineage or prominence within a community. This subchapter seeks to uncover the insidious tactics employed by Satan to undermine the lives of firstborns, drawing parallels between ancient biblical narratives where God's enemies targeted firstborns and the modern experiences that resonate with these timeless themes.

One of the most striking examples of this targeting can be found in the Book of Exodus, where Pharaoh, threatened by the growing Hebrew population, ordered the death of all male infants among the Israelites. The decree was a desperate attempt to extinguish the promise of God's people, reflecting Satan's own ambitions to thwart divine plans. Pharaoh's fear and brutality were not solely misplaced; they were a manifestation of a greater spiritual battle that had been raging long before his reign, one aimed directly at those who were set apart—the firstborns. This biblical narrative serves as a poignant reminder that firstborns, due to their unique roles and destinies, become primary targets for the adversary seeking to derail the purposes of God.

When we consider the emotional toll of such attacks, we see how they can leave lasting scars. Firstborns often feel an overwhelming sense of responsibility, believing they must be the best, to lead with authority, and to fulfill family expectations. While these traits can foster strong leadership skills, they can also morph into burdensome chains of perfectionism and fear of failure, leading to crippling anxiety when expectations are not met. The spiritual warfare initiated by the enemy might manifest in self-doubt, insecurity, and a distorted self-image, casting shadows over their identity as children of God. Similarly, we can observe the reflection of these tactics in the most chilling story of the New Testament: King Herod's decree to kill all male children under the age of two in Bethlehem. Fearful of the prophecy surrounding the birth of the Messiah, Herod felt threatened by the potential challenge to his throne and legacy, launching an attack against innocent lives. Here again, we witness a direct assault on God's plan, initiated by a ruler manipulated by fear and envy. This echoes the spiritual warfare that firstborns face today—misplaced fears that can lead them to believe they are not deserving of their identities and inheritances in Christ.

Satan employs a multi-faceted strategy to undermine the lives of firstborns, often instilling an overwhelming sense of isolation amid their struggles. In families, firstborns have the weight of being role models, peacemakers, and often the go-to figures for parental expectations. When they fail to meet these demands, which is an inevitability in the flawed human experience, they can feel like they have let not only their families down but, more dangerously, God Himself. This sense of failure can lead them into a spiral of despair, and if left unchecked, it can seriously distort their view of God's love and grace. The enemy, recognizing this vulnerability, directs arrows of condemnation, whispering lies that firstborns are not "enough"— they do not perform well enough, they do not lead well enough, and, tragically, they do not deserve to inherit God's promises.

In separating firstborns from their identity in Christ, the enemy furthers his agenda to undermine the spiritual legacy attached to their lives. Ephesians 6:12 provides clarity on this spiritual battle: "For we do not wrestle against flesh and blood, but against principalities, against powers, against the rulers of the darkness of this age, against spiritual hosts of wickedness in the heavenly places." The enemy's tactics often manifest in psychological warfare, convincing firstborns that their struggles arise from personal inadequacies rather than recognizing them as part of the broader spiritual conflict at play.

Firstborns also encounter a strategy of division, where familial conflicts are stirred up and magnified through jealousy, competition, and rivalry among siblings. This tactic harks back to the story of Cain and Abel, where the jealousy of Cain ultimately led to the first act of fratricide. Cain's anger was ignited not by mere sibling rivalry but by a demonic influence that sought to attack the future of God's covenant through Adam's lineage—an early example of how sibling rivalry can escalate beyond personal disputes into full-on spiritual warfare.

The enemy also works diligently to fuel misconceptions about what it means to be a firstborn. The societal perception that firstborns are naturally better equipped for leadership can lead to a detrimental pressure cooker environment, where only perfection and achievement are deemed acceptable. This perception can inadvertently manifest as a curse, where firstborns find themselves in constant competition against themselves, their familial expectations, and societal norms. The incessant striving for acknowledgment and validation can drive them to exhaustion, leaving room for feelings of resentment towards their roles.

Through these pressures, many firstborns grapple silently with their internal battles and spiritual resistance, convinced they are harboring weaknesses or flaws that disqualify them from God's grace. By perpetuating these false beliefs, the enemy effectively clogs firstborns' spiritual ears, making it increasingly difficult for them to hear God's voice and to recognize His promises for their lives. As believers, we must challenge these inward battles robustly, recognizing that they originate not from our shortcomings but from the adversary's desire to hinder our destinies.

Satan employs division not just among siblings but also among generations. He perpetuates the cycle of generational curses by incessantly targeting firstborns, who may unknowingly carry these burdens from their parents or grandparents. This tactic manifests through an unending cycle of shame, low self-worth, or a spirit of entitlement that can skip generations, all in pursuit of weakening the identity of future firstborns. To break free from this cycle, firstborns must first identify and confront these generational patterns, realizing that prayer and awareness are weapons in their arsenal against the enemy's schemes.

Recognizing the tactics of the enemy becomes central to the journey of all firstborns. The biblical narratives provide not only examples of the enemy's tactics but also the resilient hope that accompanies overcoming these spiritual battles. In the face of Pharaoh's decree, Moses emerged as a leader who would defy worldly expectations and liberate a nation. Similarly, the vulnerable child in Bethlehem was not merely a victim of King Herod's decree but the very embodiment of hope and redemption—the firstborn of all creation who would ultimately conquer death and sin.

To combat these tactics successfully, firstborns must actively engage in spiritual warfare. This does not merely imply a defensive posture; rather, it signifies taking the fight to the enemy. Ephesians 6:11 encourages believers to "put on the whole armor of God, that you may be able to stand against the schemes of the devil." Firstborns should embrace their identities as warriors, equipped by the truth of Scripture, infused with the courage that comes from faith, and sustained by the community that encourages their journey.

The following are practical strategies that firstborns can employ to combat these spiritual attacks. First, embracing their identity in Christ is of paramount importance. When doubts arise about their worthiness or competencies, resting in the assurance that they are loved and accepted by God can counter the enemy's lies. Understanding oneself as a beloved child of God is a powerful antidote to feelings of inadequacy.

Second, engaging in prayer and intercession serves as both a shield and a weapon. Firstborns can establish dedicated times for prayer, perhaps creating a war room in their homes where they can bring their burdens and revelations before God. Inviting trusted friends or family members to join them in prayer reinforces community support while amplifying the power of the collective prayers targeting the enemy.

Additionally, immersing themselves in Scripture is essential. Familiarizing oneself with the promises, truths, and identities laid out in the Word of God forms a firm foundation against which the enemy's deceptions can crash. Regular meditation on verses that affirm their identity—such as Romans 8:1, which proclaims there is no condemnation in Christ—can catalyze a profound internal transformation.

Further, seeking mentorship and guidance is crucial. Engaging with spiritual leaders who can provide insights, support, and wisdom will empower firstborns to withstand the enemy's schemes. This communal approach underscores the biblical principle of iron sharpening iron, reminding firstborns that they are never meant to face their battles in isolation.

In closing, identifying the tactics deployed by the enemy is integral to reclaiming the rightful identities and destinies of firstborns. Much like the ancient biblical narratives, modern firstborns encounter a multidimensional battle that requires vigilance, wisdom, and an active stance against spiritual opposition. By recognizing that the adversary does not simply attack individuals, but seeks to disrupt God-given promises, firstborns can take up their rightful roles as conquerors—standing not just in opposition to the enemy but advancing the Kingdom of God through faith, grace, and love. Empowered by their identity in Christ and bolstered by community, firstborns can emerge not just as victors against the enemy's deceptions but as bold representatives of hope and redemption in all areas of life.

CHAPTER 8

CASE STUDIES OF FIRSTBORN STRUGGLES

In the journey of life, firstborns often find themselves at the crossroads of expectations, responsibilities, and spiritual attack. This section provides a vivid exploration of real-life case studies of firstborn individuals who have faced significant challenges, showcasing their resilience amidst trials. Each story illustrates an important facet of being a firstborn, reflecting struggles that resonate deeply with many who share this unique position.

Sarah, a 30-year-old teacher, grew up in a family steeped in high expectations. As the eldest of three siblings, she became the standard-bearer for her family. Academic excellence was not just a goal; it was an unspoken expectation deeply ingrained in her childhood. When Sarah was in college, however, the weight of these expectations began to push her to the brink of burnout. Despite her good grades, she constantly felt like she was losing the battle for her family's approval.

"I remember sitting in my dorm room," she recalls, "feeling completely alone. My parents always praised my younger siblings for their achievements, while I felt like I was still trying to prove myself. I started to doubt my worth, thinking, 'Am I not enough?'" The turning point for Sarah came when she sought counseling. In therapy, she learned to confront the unrealistic standards imposed by her upbringing. Embracing her faith, Sarah found solace in the Bible, particularly in Romans 8:1, which states, "Therefore, there is now no condemnation for those who are in Christ Jesus." This realization led her to understand that her identity is rooted in Christ, and not in her achievements.

As Sarah navigated her journey, she discovered the importance of sharing her struggles with fellow firstborns. "We need each other," she emphasizes. "Having a community who understands your battles can lighten the load."

Mark's story parallels Sarah's in many ways yet channels a different kind of challenge. At 28, he stepped into the role of caretaker when his parents divorced. As the firstborn son, Mark felt the responsibility of keeping the family together weigh heavily on him. Nights spent comforting his siblings turned into days filled with anxiety. "Honestly, I was overwhelmed. I had to hold things together while dealing with my own sense of loss and betrayal," he shares. "It felt like all eyes were on me, expecting me to be strong, when inside I was crumbling."

Mark's crisis came to a head when he faced a serious health scare, which he later realized was triggered by the stress he had been carrying. It was only through a combination of prayer, family support, and connecting with a men's group at church that he began to heal. "I learned that it's okay to seek help and not always have the answers. My role as a firstborn does not mean I have to shoulder everything alone."

His experience revealed that the adversary's strategy can often lead firstborns to internalize pain, believing that vulnerability equates to weakness. Mark found strength in expressing his struggles, encouraging others to do the same. "It's through our stories that we find healing," he states.

Laura, a vibrant young professional, faced a different kind of battle; hers was rooted in the competitive corporate world. As a firstborn daughter in a family of overachievers, she found herself striving for promotion, often battling feelings of inferiority. "I always felt like I had to outdo my siblings, and the workplace only amplified that pressure," she confesses.

Her turning point came when she faced harsh criticism from a supervisor. This experience shattered her confidence, pushing her into a cycle of self-doubt and anxiety. "I would lay awake at night, replaying every mistake in my head. I kept hearing the enemy's voice telling me I wasn't cut out for this," she remembers.

Realizing she couldn't Face this alone, Laura turned to her faith and leaned on her church community. Through mentoring relationships and prayer, she found renewed strength. "I learned to redefine success. It wasn't about outshining my siblings; it was about being faithful with what God had given me."

Laura's victory was not simply in overcoming workplace challenges, but in cultivating a sense of self-worth. Now, she uses her experiences to mentor other young professionals, emphasizing the importance of authenticity over perfection. "We're not defined by our roles or titles," she asserts. "We must remember our true identity is in Christ."

The narratives of Sarah, Mark, and Laura encapsulate key pressures faced by many firstborns, including familial expectations, care responsibilities, and workplace competition. Their stories resonate with the silence that often accompanies struggles unique to firstborns. They illustrate how societal and familial pressures can manifest as attacks from the enemy, driving these individuals toward spiritual warfare.

Paul's story adds another layer to this exploration. As a musician, he faced immense pressure to excel while covering the artistic endeavors of his younger siblings. "Music has always been my passion, but as the firstborn, the burden felt heavy," he explains. "There was an invisible bar set, and it felt impossible to reach."

When Paul failed to secure a record deal, he spiraled into disappointment. "In my mind, I was not just failing as a musician; I was failing as the eldest son," he says. In this dark time, he began to notice the enemy's depression lurking in the shadows, feeding on his insecurities and driving a wedge between him and his faith.

Paul's saving grace came through seeking out prayer groups and creative communities where he could express his fears freely. "I learned that vulnerability breeds authenticity. It's okay to admit when you're struggling, especially when you're a firstborn," he shares.

Revealing his battles became transformative for him. Paul's willingness to share his journey paved the way for others in his community to do the same. "It's powerful—it creates a bond of trust. We're all navigating similar struggles as firstborns."

Another significant aspect is the tension firstborns often feel when stepping into leadership roles. Many view these positions as both an honor and a heavy burden, creating environments ripe for spiritual warfare.

Consider Rachel, a school principal who became the youngest in the district to secure her position. As a firstborn, Rachel inherited a legacy of leadership within her family that set the stage for her career. However, the pressure to maintain this legacy was stifling. "I didn't just feel like I had to be successful; I felt like my family's reputation rested on my shoulders," she reflects. "Every decision felt like it was a mark against my family's name."

Despite an impressive start, she encountered criticism, which eroded her confidence. The burden of expectations transformed into a spiritual attack, shackling her in anxiety and self-doubt. Denise, her mentor, encouraged her to find refuge in prayer, turning every anxious thought into a supplication.

"Learning to surrender my fears to God was liberating," Rachel conveys. "Worship became my weapon against the lies that I believed."

As Rachel began to foster a supportive culture among her staff, she found healing in the community. By sharing her experiences and encouraging open dialogue, she broke the chains of isolation that often bind firstborns.

The stories of these firstborns illuminate their battles, revealing how they confront the adversary's tactics. Each narrative serves not only as a personal journey but also as an encouraging testimony to others grappling with similar battles.

As firstborns share their struggles, they foster an environment that normalizes vulnerability, allowing others to draw strength from shared experiences. The emotional depth expressed in these narratives underscores not only the individual challenges encountered but also emphasizes the importance of recognizing these struggles as integral parts of the spiritual battle.

These firstborns remind us that it's within vulnerability that we find strength and community. They exemplify how sharing struggles can form bonds that transcend individual experiences, reinforcing a sense of belonging in the face of spiritual warfare.

Communicating their challenges, firstborns collectively shed light on the tactics of the enemy, exposing how these attacks can infiltrate various facets of life. Recognizing the patterns of these attacks is crucial in building resilience among firstborns and creating supportive environments where they can thrive.

The testimony of these individuals serves as a clarion call to acknowledge the unique battles faced by firstborns. It emphasizes that these struggles are not isolated incidents but common experiences that warrant communal response.

As Sarah, Mark, Laura, Paul, and Rachel have shown, navigating the trials of being a firstborn is not merely a personal story of triumph but a shared journey that resonates deeply with those walking similar paths. By embracing their challenges, they cultivate connections that transcend their individual experiences, establishing a united front against the adversarial forces targeting firstborns.

In this way, the spiritual battle becomes an empowering narrative of resilience, community, and faith—a powerful testimony that reminds firstborns they are not alone in their struggles, but part of a larger story of hope and victory through Christ.

CHAPTER 9

THE PATH TO EMPOWERMENT

The weight of being a firstborn is an experience shared by many who carry the burden of expectations, responsibilities, and, often, spiritual attacks that seem aimed directly at them. It is crucial for firstborns to realize that they are not alone in this battle and that there are practical steps they can take to empower themselves against the spiritual challenges they face. This subchapter will outline actionable strategies that firstborns can utilize to defend themselves against the schemes of the enemy, fostering a profound sense of empowerment and resilience through their faith.

One of the foremost tools at a firstborn's disposal is the power of prayer. Prayer is not merely a ritualistic practice; it is a dynamic conversation with God that can shape realities. For firstborns, establishing a consistent prayer life is essential in combating feelings of inadequacy and insecurity that spiritual attacks often exacerbate. In prayer, firstborns find a sanctuary where they can lay bare their concerns, fears, and aspirations before God, seeking both guidance and strength.

Start by setting aside dedicated time for prayer each day, whether in the morning to start the day with intention or in the evening to reflect on the day. Create a prayer journal that allows you to document your thoughts, prayers, and the responses you sense from God. Writing down these experiences can deepen your connection with God and remind you of His faithfulness.

Incorporate specific prayers that address your unique battles. For example, if you struggle against feelings of inadequacy, pray passages from Scripture that affirm your identity in Christ, such as Romans

8:37, which states, "In all these things we are more than conquerors through Him who loved us." By anchoring your prayers in Scripture, you establish a firm foundation that counteracts the lies the enemy may attempt to feed you.

Scripture meditation is another powerful strategy in the firstborn's arsenal. Just as physical nourishment is necessary for bodily strength, spiritual nourishment is vital for resilience against spiritual warfare. Meditating on Scripture involves not only reading but also reflecting deeply on the verses, allowing them to permeate your mind and heart.

Select verses that speak to your identity and purpose as a firstborn. For instance, Ephesians 1:5 reminds us that we are adopted as children of God through Jesus Christ. Internalizing the truth of this adoption can combat feelings of loneliness and unworthiness that often accompany firstborn status. Create a habit of memorizing key verses that resonate with your spirit. When spiritual attacks arise, having these verses readily accessible equips you to counter the enemy's schemes with truth.

Consider establishing a "verse of the week" practice, where you choose a particular scripture to meditate on each week. Reflect on its meaning throughout your day and how it applies to your life as a firstborn. Encourage other firstborns in your community to join you in this practice for mutual support and accountability, allowing each person to share insights and revelations gained from their meditation.

While personal prayer and meditation are crucial, it is equally important to recognize the significance of community support. Isolation can be a breeding ground for doubt and confusion, particularly for firstborns who may feel the weight of expectations alone. Engaging in a community of like-minded believers provides a support system that can uplift and strengthen you in moments of vulnerability.

Seek out opportunities to connect with fellow firstborns, whether through church groups, Bible studies, or fellowship through shared activities. Establishing these relationships offers a space to share experiences, pray for one another, and share insights into overcoming challenges. Support groups not only encourage emotional well- being but also reinforce the sense that your struggles are shared, reducing feelings of isolation.

Incorporate regular gatherings where firstborns can openly discuss their journeys. Create a safe environment where vulnerability is encouraged, and prayer for one another becomes a central component of each meeting. Hearing others share their stories of struggle and victory can kindle hope and inspire you to overcome your challenges.

As you navigate the path to empowerment, it's essential to remember the sovereignty of God. The Bible is replete with stories of individuals who faced immense challenges and attacks yet emerged victorious through their faith. Consider the story of David, who, as a young shepherd, encountered the towering giant, Goliath. Armed only with faith and a few stones, David confronted his adversary, echoing the power of trusting in God over his fears. Reflecting on such biblical narratives can serve as a source of encouragement, reminding you that you have the authority to confront spiritual attacks just as David did. Philippians 4:13 declares, "I can do all things through Christ who strengthens me." This verse goes beyond mere affirmation; it empowers firstborns to recognize that their strength lies not in their own abilities but in a relationship with Christ.

Faith is the cornerstone of resilience. As firstborns, embodying a faith-filled mindset helps combat feelings of doubt. Construct daily affirmations that remind you of your identity in Christ. For instance, declare each morning, "I am a beloved child of God." This simple yet profound affirmation reinforces the truth of your worth and purpose, strengthening your resolve against enemy attacks.

Moreover, surround yourself with accountability partners who can encourage you in your faith journey. These individuals can help you maintain focus and unity in your goals as firstborns. Engaging in discussions that challenge and uplift each other spurs spiritual growth, as you pray together and share insights gleaned from Scripture.

In addition to prayer, scripture meditation, and community support, firstborns can find empowerment through acts of service. Engaging actively in your community fosters a strong sense of purpose and identity.

Consider volunteering in programs that uplift others: mentoring younger individuals, serving at local charities, or participating in outreach initiatives at your church.

Through service, you not only provide support to others but also reinforce your identity as a firstborn with a divine mission. Serving alongside others builds camaraderie and deepens your connection with both God and the people around you. The acts of kindness and love you share reflect the character of Christ, which can counteract feelings of negativity or doubt.

A vital component of the path to empowerment is recognizing and wielding the authority you have as a believer. You possess the spiritual authority to resist the enemy and claim victory over the attacks that aim to steal your joy and purpose. James 4:7 tells us, "Submit yourselves, then, to God. Resist the devil, and he will flee from you." This verse summarizes the need for submission to God's will while actively resisting spiritual warfare.

Affirm your authority regularly through prayer, declaring your freedom from spiritual bondage. Engage in spiritual warfare through the power of Jesus' name, using your voice to resist the enemy's lies. Utilize declarations based on scripture, such as, "I am redeemed by the blood of the Lamb," reinforcing your position as a child of God. As you implement these actionable steps, it is essential to remain steadfast in your faith amid adversity. The enemy may present challenges that seem insurmountable, but your foundation in Christ will sustain you. Establish a practice of gratitude where you acknowledge the blessings in your life, even during difficult times.

Cultivating gratitude shifts your focus from the struggles to the abundant grace of God.

Keep in mind that the path to empowerment is not a one-time journey but a continual process of growth and development. Embrace your progress, recognizing that each step taken toward empowerment is a testament to your resilience and faith. Reflect on your journey periodically, identifying areas for improvement and celebrating both big and small.

Finally, conclude this subchapter with a message of hope, reminding all firstborns that though they may face challenges, they are equipped with the tools necessary to overcome. The objective is not merely to resist attacks but to thrive in their identity as children of God.

Stand firm in the knowledge that you are not defined by your struggles but empowered by your identity in Christ. As you embark on this journey toward empowerment, trust in God's perfect plan and timing, knowing that the battle belongs to Him.

In the face of adversity, declare your authority, embrace your identity, engage in prayer, meditate on scripture, seek community support, and serve with purpose. These steps not only safeguard against spiritual attacks but also build a life marked by empowerment and victory. Stand firm, firstborns, for you are more than conquerors, and the journey ahead is filled with hope and possibilities.

CHAPTER 10

THE FIRSTBORN OF ALL CREATION

Understanding Colossians 1:15

Colossians 1:15 presents a profound statement about Jesus Christ, referring to Him as the "Firstborn of all creation." This designation carries immense theological significance, inviting us to delve deeply into its meaning and implications. In a world filled with a myriad of challenges and struggles, particularly impacting firstborns, understanding the identity and authority of Christ as the ultimate firstborn becomes essential. By unpacking this scripture, we are not only given insights into the nature of Jesus but also provided a transformative lens through which contemporary firstborns can view their lives and purpose.

The term "firstborn" in the context of Colossians 1:15 does not merely point to Jesus' chronological place in history or His earthly lineage. Instead, it reflects His preeminence in creation and His unique relationship with the Father. The Greek word used here, "prototokos," holds a rich meaning that extends beyond birth order. It encapsulates the idea of supremacy, authority, and inheritance. In biblical times, the firstborn had critical responsibilities and rights within the family. This biblical framework is essential as we examine Christ's role and what it means for firstborns today.

To fully grasp the significance of this title, we must also consider the context of the Colossian church to which Paul was writing. The letter to the Colossians was addressed to a community struggling with various theological influences, including Gnosticism, which sought to undermine the supremacy of Christ. In response, Paul emphasizes not only that Jesus is the Firstborn of all creation but also that He is the image of the invisible God, the Creator of all things. By articulating Christ's divine nature and authority, Paul validates the faith of the believers, urging them to resist any false teachings that would diminish who Jesus is.

One critical aspect of understanding Christ as the "Firstborn of all creation" is recognizing His role in creation itself. Colossians 1:16-17 further elaborates on this by declaring that all things were created through Him and for Him. This speaks to the active involvement of Christ in the creation process, indicating that He is not a distant figure but intimately connected to all that exists. His role as Creator underscores His divine authority; nothing was made without Him. For firstborns who often grapple with feelings of being overlooked or burdened by expectations, recognizing that they are connected to the One who created the universe can be a source of profound comfort and purpose.

Moreover, the understanding of Jesus as the "Firstborn" positions Him as one who embodies the hope and redemption necessary for all firstborns. Throughout the biblical narrative, the concept of the firstborn is fraught with both blessing and significant challenges. From Cain and Abel to Isaac and Ishmael, the biblical accounts often showcase the trials that firstborns endure due to the higher expectations placed upon them. However, in Jesus, we find the ultimate resolution to these struggles. He embodies the perfect firstborn, the one who not only confronts the weight of expectation but also redeems and redefines it through His sacrifice.

Exploring the transformative implications of Jesus' identity as the firstborn provides contemporary firstborns with a mirror through which they can reflect on their personal struggles and spiritual journeys. Many firstborns often feel the weight of responsibility, perfectionism, and societal expectations bearing down upon them. Understanding that Christ, as the Firstborn, has walked the path of suffering and victory offers a liberating perspective. This means that while they may face challenges, they are not alone—there is a Savior who fully comprehends the unique struggles inherent in their role.

Moreover, Jesus' identity as the firstborn extends beyond merely reflecting His preeminence in creation; it also signifies the intimate relationship He has with God the Father. This familial connection invites firstborns to see themselves as children of God, adopted into a royal family. They share in the inheritance provided through Christ's redemptive work. This spiritual inheritance is a powerful counternarrative to the feelings of inadequacy and isolation that firstborns may experience in their earthly families. By recognizing their true identity in Christ, firstborns can find strength and empowerment to fulfill their divine purpose.

As we continue to delve into the passage, it is essential to acknowledge the cultural significance of the title "firstborn." In ancient Jewish culture, the concept of firstborn held profound importance, being closely linked to themes of blessing, leadership, and divine favor. For instance, the firstborn sons were typically seen as the carriers of their family's legacy, often being granted a double portion of the inheritance. By linking this cultural understanding of firstborns to Christ, believers are invited to embrace the richness of their spiritual inheritance and consider the responsibilities it entails. Furthermore, as we reflect on the struggles of firstborns today, we must also acknowledge the societal pressures that accompany this identity.

The expectations for firstborns to excel academically, take on leadership roles, or consistently set an example for younger siblings can create an environment of intense pressure and anxiety. However, the message of Colossians 1:15 serves as a reminder that despite these challenges, there exists a promise of hope and redemption through Jesus Christ. He understands their struggles and invites them to lean into His grace, which is sufficient for their weaknesses. This understanding can transform how firstborns view their own narratives. Instead of seeing themselves as mere victims of expectation, they can reclaim their stories as a journey marked by the redemptive power of Christ.

The identity of the firstborn is one that can be filled with grace and love rather than burden and shame. It allows for a new perspective that aligns personal struggles with the greater narrative of redemption unfolding throughout scripture.

In practical terms, this connection to Jesus as the Firstborn also encourages contemporary firstborns to engage in active discipleship and community. Just as Jesus came to serve rather than to be served, firstborns are called to embody this spirit of servanthood in their families and communities. This can manifest in mentorship relationships, volunteer opportunities, or simply by being a supportive presence for others facing similar challenges. By taking on this role, firstborns can step into their identity and purpose as agents of transformation in their spheres of influence.

Additionally, studying Colossians 1:15 invites firstborns to reflect on their worth and identity separate from societal expectations. The world often defines value based on achievements, accolades, or status. However, in Christ as the Firstborn, they find their worth deeply rooted in being cherished children of God. This freedom can liberate firstborns from the relentless pursuit of perfection and allow them to embrace their unique gifts and callings, trusting that their value is not dependent on their performance but instead on their relationship with Christ.

As we consider the overarching narrative of the Bible, we see that the theme of firstborns is not limited to individual stories. Instead, it underscores a larger cosmic narrative of redemption that culminates in Christ's work on the cross. Jesus, as the Firstborn, not only takes on the challenges associated with that title but also transforms the meaning of what it means to be a firstborn in the family of God. He reconnects the broken relationship between humanity and God that began in the Garden of Eden, offering a pathway to reconciliation and wholeness.

For firstborns wrestling with feelings of inadequacy or struggle, the message of Colossians 1:15 is inherently reassuring. They are part of a larger family that extends beyond earthly ties, marked by the blood of Christ. His authority as the Firstborn transcends temporal struggles and speaks directly to the heart of who they are and who they are meant to be. Understanding this spiritual heritage and its implications empowers firstborns to rise above their circumstances and embrace the promises of God.

In considering how Jesus, the ultimate Firstborn, impacts the identity of contemporary firstborns, we must address the journey of understanding and acceptance. It can be challenging for firstborns to reconcile their roles with the reality of their struggles and the expectations of those around them. They may feel isolated or burdened by the responsibilities placed upon them. However, there is an invitation to journey alongside Christ, embracing both their challenges and their identity as beloved children of God.

Moreover, through Christ's example, firstborns are encouraged to champion the significance of community and support among one another. This invitation is to forge bonds that celebrate shared experiences and collectively lift each other in faith. The sense of tribe that emerges among firstborns, recognizing their unique struggles and the redemptive power of Christ together, can foster resilience and hope.

As we conclude this exploration of Colossians 1:15, it is vital to reflect on the implications of Jesus being the "Firstborn of all creation." For firstborns today, the promise of hope, redemption, and identity is not merely a theological assertion but a living truth that can transform their lives. By understanding their connection to Christ, they can rewrite the narrative of their lives with faith and confidence.

Ultimately, being a firstborn is a divine calling, underscored by the grace and authority found in Jesus Christ. It invites them to embrace their identity, recognizing their unique purpose within the larger story of God's redemption. As they navigate their journeys, firstborns can find solace in Christ's redemptive work, knowing that they are not alone. Each of their struggles is an opportunity for growth, purpose, and deeper intimacy with their Creator, the Firstborn of all creation. As they embrace their identities, they contribute to the narrative of redemption that is ongoing and active in the world around them, heralding a future filled with hope, purpose, and victory.

CHAPTER 11

JESUS' SACRIFICE AS THE ULTIMATE REDEMPTION

In the endless narrative of human existence, within the overarching tapestry of creation, there lies the pivotal moment of redemption birthed at the foot of the cross. As we contemplate Jesus' role as the Firstborn of all creation, we come to understand that His existence is not merely a point of origin but a profound embodiment of divine purpose that extends into the realm of salvation. This is particularly significant for firstborns, who often carry an inherent weight of expectation, responsibility, and scrutiny. For them, the redemptive power of Christ's sacrifice transcends the physical, transforming it into a spiritual liberation that invites all to step into the fullness of their identity in Him.

As firstborns, many individuals navigate life with a unique set of pressures and burdens. Cultural expectations shape their roles, often demanding they be high achievers, leaders, and caretakers. The weight of responsibility may settle heavily upon their shoulders, leading to feelings of inadequacy, anxiety, and self-doubt. Many firstborns might find themselves ensnared in the belief that they must earn love and approval through their achievements. These challenges can breed a deep sense of isolation and the haunting specter of failure. It is within this backdrop that the significance of Jesus' sacrifice becomes exceedingly clear—He offers not just hope but a path to liberation from these burdens.

The Bible presents Jesus not merely as a historical figure but as the essence of divine love poured out for mankind. Colossians 1:15-20 illustrates that He is the image of the invisible God, the firstborn over all creation. This designation as "firstborn" goes beyond chronology; it conveys authority, status, and a special relationship with the Father.

As the Firstborn, Jesus embodies the ideal Sonship that humanity was meant to experience, exemplifying unblemished obedience, unwavering faith, and profound love. Through His life, we see the manifest character of God, which should inspire every firstborn to re-evaluate their own identities in the light of this ultimate example. The act of sacrifice on the cross stands as the crux of Jesus' mission and the fulcrum upon which the redemptive story pivots. The weight of sin, which permeated humanity after the fall, demanded a sacrifice unlike any other. Jesus, in His infinite love, willingly took upon Himself the sins of the world, extending grace to all who would accept Him. As we reflect on this, it is essential to understand that His sacrifice was not merely about atonement but also about restoration. God desires His children to walk in wholeness, free from the shackles of past mistakes and burdens.

Consider the story of Sarah, a firstborn grappling with the pressures of family expectations. As the eldest, she was accustomed to setting the standard for her siblings. Her parents, though well-meaning, often praised her achievements while inadvertently neglecting to affirm her intrinsic worth. Over time, Sarah began to equate her value with her performance, leading to a cycle of perfectionism that left her exhausted and anxious. In moments of despair, she felt distant from God, believing her failures disqualified her from His love and forgiveness. It wasn't until she encountered the message of redemption through Christ's sacrifice that everything changed. By embracing her identity in Jesus, she realized her worth was not contingent upon what she accomplished. Instead, it was rooted in the unchanging love of Christ demonstrated by His willingness to die for her, sinful and imperfect as she was. This understanding granted Sarah the freedom she so desperately sought, allowing her to step into her own identity as a beloved daughter of the King, rather than merely a performer seeking approval.

Every firstborn has a story—a tapestry woven from unique struggles, triumphs, and internal battles. These narratives collectively echo the broader redemption story found in the gospel. When Jesus proclaimed on thecross, "It is finished," He dismantled the foundation of guilt and shame that binds individuals to their perceived failures. The cross becomes not just a symbol of suffering but of victory, a transformative exchange where our sinfulness meets divine grace. It bridges the chasm created by the Fall, offering reconciliation and a fresh start to all who will accept this gift.

In Ephesians 1:5, we read of being predestined for adoption as His children through Jesus Christ. This powerful truth reshapes our understanding of familial dynamics. Many firstborns have experienced pressures that make them feel as though they must prove their worth to gain acceptance and love, not only from their families but also from God. However, the stunning reality of the gospel is this: God does not call us to perform for His love; rather, He invites us into a relationship based on grace. In Christ, every firstborn is not just another member of the family but an heir, valued and cherished regardless of their past.

Let us look at Luke 15, the parable of the Prodigal Son, and consider the older brother's perspective. This figure, often overshadowed by the younger brother's reckless journey, wrestles with resentment and entitlement. He embodies the pressures faced by many firstborns, diligent, obedient, yet estranged from the joy of grace. When he refuses to join in the celebration of his brother's return, he expresses his feelings of inadequacy and misunderstanding of the father's love. The father's response, inviting him to come and share in the joy, is a reminder that grace is available for all, regardless of their journey. This parable becomes a beautiful illustration of how Jesus' redemptive work is accessible to every firstborn, inviting them to relinquish the weight of expectation and embrace their identity as part of the family of God.

Redemptionis not a one-time occurrence but an ongoing engagement in the life of every believer. As firstborns reflect on their identities and navigate their unique struggles, they must remember that Jesus' sacrifice serves as a continual invitation to restoration. Each day presents an opportunity to surrender the burdens of yesterday and walk in the freedom that He offers. This freedom allows firstborns to redefine success—not as achieving a checklist of accomplishments but as a journey of faith, trust, and reliance on God's grace.

The transformation that comes through mbraceng Jesus' sacrifice does not happen in isolation. Community plays a crucial role in the journey of healing and restoration, particularly for firstborns. Sharing testimonies and journeys within supportive circles can ignite hope and foster understanding. As individuals recount their struggles and victories, they illuminate the redemptive power of Christ at work in their lives, reinforcing the truth that no one is alone in their battles. The prevailing darkness of isolation can be shattered through the light of shared experiences, encouraging firstborns to lean on one another as they navigate the complexities of their roles.

Moreover, the significance of Christ's sacrifice is amplified in the context of communal worship and accountability. Engaging in a community of believers allows firstborns to search their hearts and confront insecurities with trusted allies. As others surround them with encouragement and accountability, they can find healing in a safe space—one where they are reminded of their worth and potential in Christ. In these gatherings, the narrative of Christ's sacrifice is echoed, fortifying their faith and reinforcing the message of hope that permeates the gospel.

Jesus' sacrifice also imparts a transformative power that enables firstborns to extend grace to others. As they experience the depth of Jesus' love for them, they are compelled to share this gift with those around them. It inspires not only a sense of belonging but also ignites their purpose—to become instruments of healing and reconciliation in a world longing for truth. The burden of expectation that weighs so heavily might fuel the desire to hoard love and approval; however, recognizing the eternal grace bestowed through Jesus encourages firstborns to release this grasping tendency. They can step into the calling of serving others, ushering in hope and healing forged at the cross.

Let us take a moment to reflect on Jacob, another firstborn whose journey epitomizes the redemptive power of Christ's sacrifice. For Jacob, life was characterized by pressure to perform and fulfill the roles that society predetermined. Growing up amid familial expectations and success, he ultimately found himself entangled in a web of unhealthy comparisons, and when he fell short, shame flooded in. His moment of turning came when he discovered the depth of Jesus' love through scripture—he read the passage in Romans 8, affirming that nothing could separate him from the love of God. In embracing this truth, Jacob encountered an unprecedented freedom. Rather than striving to meet imposed expectations, he found peace in resting within his identity as a beloved son of the King. This transformative understanding empowered him to encourage others trapped in performance-driven mindsets to experience the same grace that set him free.

As firstborns reflect on their own identities, they should ask: How does Jesus' sacrifice reshape my understanding of who I am? How does it give me courage to walk free from the pressures that try to bind me? This introspection fosters a deeper relationship with Christ, allowing individuals to experience the transformative grace that shapes their journey. In doing so, they are not only set free from the pressures of expectation but also unleashed to soar in the knowledge of their identity within God's family.

Jesus' role as the Firstborn of all creation serves as a critical reminder that He is intimately aware of the struggles firstborns face. Whether the sense of continuous striving, the burden of responsibility, or the desire for approval, He intimately understands the nuances of these experiences. His sacrifice illustrates that freedom is attainable, and that the way to find healing lies in embracing His love and restoration. In conclusion, as firstborns engage with the story of redemption through Jesus, they realize that their struggles do not define or limit them. Instead, they are empowered to rise above familial expectations, societal pressures, and their own insecurities.

The cross stands as a beacon of hope, a compelling testament to the depths of divine love that invites them into freedom. Embracing

Jesus—His sacrifice, His grace, and His identity—will ultimately lead firstborns into lives marked by healing, purpose, and unrelenting love. There, they can rest in who they are created to be, knowing that they are cherished firstborns not just in earthly terms but as sons and daughters, heirs of an everlasting legacy, eternally loved by their Heavenly Father.

CHAPTER 12

LIVING AS THE FIRSTBORN'S HEIRS

As we journey deeper into the heart of God's narrative, we come face to face with a profound truth: firstborns carry within them the incredible identity of being heirs to God's promises. Embracing this identity opens a pathway to understanding our role as adopted children in God's family. For those of us who identify as firstborns, this realization is not merely a theological assertion; it is a living legacy that defines who we are and shapes our destinies.

To grasp the significance of our inheritance in Christ, we must first understand the concept of adoption as articulated in Scripture. The Apostle Paul writes in Ephesians 1:5, "He predestined us for adoption to sonship through Jesus Christ, by his pleasure and will." Here, Paul emphasizes that our adoption into God's family is intentional—it was predestined. This truth is deeply liberating, as it reminds us that our place within God's family does not hinge on our merit or performance, but rather on His divine choice and love. Being a firstborn comes with unique expectations, pressures, and sometimes the shadows of comparison and rivalry. However, the beauty of our identity as heirs alleviates those burdens, allowing us to redefine our roles in the light of God's grace. In a world where competition often reigns, and familial hierarchies can impose restrictive definitions of success, we are invited to step into our inheritance as children of the King—a status that transcends any earthly expectations.

Consider the parable of the prodigal son in Luke 15:11-32. In this timeless narrative, we encounter both a younger son, who squanders his inheritance, and an older brother, who struggles with feelings of resentment and entitlement. The older brother embodies the weight of expectations placed on firstborns, grappling with the harsh reality that sometimes our understanding of inheritance may lead us to isolation rather than intimacy. Yet, the father's response reveals the heart of God: "You are always with me, and everything I have is yours" (Luke 15:31). Here, we see a glimpse of our inheritance— not merely material wealth, but a deep, relational connection with our Father who invites us to embrace the fullness of our identity.

In personal testimony, we can find affirmation of what it means to live as heirs. Take Sarah, a firstborn from a large family, who often felt the pressure of perfection associated with her birth order. She excelled academically and was her parents' pride, yet the quiet weight of fulfilling expectations became a heavy burden. It wasn't until she experienced a personal relationship with Christ that her perspective shifted. Embracing her identity as an heir to God's promises, she found freedom in the understanding that her value was rooted not in her achievements but in her being—a beloved daughter of the King. This profound truth released her from striving and opened her heart to grace, propelling her into a life marked by acceptance and community.

Similarly, consider David, another firstborn who once felt lost in the shadow of his younger siblings' accomplishments. As he struggled to find his own path while wrestling with comparison, he encountered the transformative power of understanding his identity in Christ. During a challenging season, he learned that his place at the table was secure and that being an heir to God's promises meant stepping into a legacy of hope rather than living as a mere reflection of family expectations. As he surrendered his insecurities to God, David discovered a community of firstborns who shared similar struggles, where they could encourage and uplift one another—a true demonstration of the church as God's family.

The invitation to step into our roles as heirs is intricately tied to our understanding of inheritance. In Romans 8:17, Paul further confirms this identity by stating, "Now if we are children, then we are heirs— heirs of God and co-heirs with Christ." This powerful declaration expands our perspective beyond mere inheritance; it positions us as co-heirs with Christ Himself. Jesus, the firstborn over all creation, willingly shares His inheritance with us, including the promise of eternal life and the blessings of His kingdom.

Moreover, understanding our role as heirs implies an active participation in God's mission. We are called not just to receive but also to reflect the character of our Father—to be agents of grace, love, and truth in a world desperately in need of good news. Our identity compels us to move beyond self-centeredness and to contribute to the collective story of God's family. This calling involves embracing our unique gifts and strengths as we seek to serve others, realizing that true fulfillment comes when we embody Christ's love within our communities.

As firstborns, we often find ourselves in leading roles, which can inadvertently reinforce the myth that our worth is contingent upon our ability to lead and succeed. However, being an heir in God's family debunks this myth, revealing that our worth is inherently linked to our identity as children of God. We are not defined by our responsibilities or accomplishments but rather by our relationship with Him. This understanding transforms how we lead, as it encourages us to do so from a place of humility rather than obligation.

Within the context of our heritage as heirs, we also carry the responsibility of carrying forward our family legacies. Ephesians 3:20-21 reminds us that God can do immeasurably more than we ask or imagine, according to His power that is at work within us. Our inheritance is not merely a static gift; it is a dynamic force meant to fuel our service and outreach in the world. As firstborns, we possess an unparalleled opportunity to leverage our positions within our families and communities to impart the values and wisdom of our faith to the next generation.

In reflecting on what it means to truly live as heirs, we must also confront the apprehensions and doubts that may arise. So often, we allow the shadows of insecurity and fear to overshadow our understanding of our rightful place. In moments of doubt, let us heed the words of 1 Peter 2:9: "But you are a chosen people, a royal priesthood, a holy nation, God's special possession." This passage reaffirms our identity, encouraging us to rise above doubts and to recognize the authority granted to us as firstborns. Embracing this truth liberates us to embody our calling fully.

Furthermore, the narrative woven throughout Scripture of God's steadfast love for the marginalized and the lost serves to remind us of our responsibility to advocate for those who may struggle with their identities. As heirs of His promises, we are called to stand in the gap, ministering to others as we ourselves have been ministered to. We carry the charge to actively engage with the world around us, to identify and share our stories of redemption, and to acknowledge the work God has done in our lives.

As this subchapter ends, we invite you to consider how you can embrace your identity as an heir in Christ. Reflect on the legacy you will leave behind, not only as a firstborn but also as a member of God's family. We are encouraged to engage with one another, fostering connections that deepen our understanding of what it truly means to belong. From being heirs to being a blessing to others, we are challenged to live out the hope and purpose that God exhibits in our lives.

In closing, remember that our journey as firstborns is interwoven with the hope found in Christ. We no longer need to shoulder the burden of expectations or the need to prove ourselves. Instead, we are invited to celebrate our inheritance and our identity as ambassadors of His kingdom. By embracing the fullness of this identity, we empower ourselves to contribute to a legacy that spurs us toward love, service, and transformation. Let us step boldly into our roles as heirs, knowing that we are held securely in a family where the love of the Father overflows, urging us to share that abundance with a world in need.

CHAPTER 13

REDEMPTION AND RESTORATION

The Power of Acceptance

Embracing acceptance is a powerful journey for anyone striving to understand their place in the world, but for firstborns, this journey is steeped in the weight of expectation and responsibility. From a young age, firstborns often find themselves at the center of family dynamics, tasked with meeting the standards set by parents, relatives, and even society at large. These pressures can lead to feelings of inadequacy, anxiety, and a longing for validation, which in turn may cloud their perception of identity and purpose.

However, acceptance in Christ presents atransformative opportunity for firstborns to step into a new identity, one founded on grace rather than performance. This acceptance not only alleviates the burdens of expectation but also empowers firstborns to recognize their inherent value as children of God. In this subchapter, we will explore the profound impact of accepting Christ, highlighting testimonies of those who have undergone significant changes through their acceptance of faith. This narrative will emphasize humility and trust as essential elements in understanding and navigating the journey of faith.

The journey to acceptance often begins with self-awareness—the recognition of one's struggles and shortcomings. Many firstborns grapple with challenges unique to their role; they tend to carry fears and insecurities tied to their position within the family. The weight of expectation can morph into a relentless drive for perfection, often at the expense of their emotional and spiritual well-being. They may wrestle with questions like: Am I good enough? Will I ever meet my parents' expectations? Have I disappointed those who depend on me? Such questions can be debilitating, creating a cycle of striving those distances them from the unconditional love and acceptance offered by Christ.

The first step in this journey of acceptance is to acknowledge these struggles openly. This might involve a moment of introspection, where firstborns examine the narratives, they have constructed about themselves based on external expectations. It may be uncomfortable to confront these realities, but this process is essential for genuine growth and healing. By laying bare their vulnerabilities, firstborns can begin to experience the freedom that comes from humility. They are reminded that admitting struggles is not a sign of weakness, but rather a courageous step towards spiritual maturity.

As firstborns begin to surrender their burdens to God, they may find the comforting truths of scripture that affirm their identities as beloved children. In Ephesians 1:4-5, it is written, "For he chose us in him before the foundation of the world, that we should be holy and blameless before him. In love, he predestined us for adoption to himself as sons through Jesus Christ, according to the purpose of his will." These words reveal a profound reality—that their worth is not contingent upon their performance or adherence to expectations but is deeply rooted in God's unconditional love.

Transformational stories often arise in the contexts of acceptance. Take Sarah, a firstborn who felt an immense weight to become the family's success story. For years, she pursued academic excellence and career ambition at the expense of her mental health. Struggling with anxiety and a lack of fulfillment, Sarah found herself caught in a cyclical pattern of striving and disappointment. It wasn't until she hit rock bottom—feeling lost and alone—that she encountered a community of faith. Through prayer and conversations with others who understood her burdens, Sarah began to understand the concept of grace and the meaning of true acceptance.

In that environment, Sarah discovered the transformative power of accepting Christ. She learned that it was okay to be imperfect, to struggle, and to be on a journey rather than achieving a destination. Her faith became a source of strength, helping her embrace her failures and shortcomings without shame. Sarah's story resonates with many firstborns who may fear their inadequacies. Her acceptance of Christ opened pathways to healing and restoration, allowing her to redefine success on her terms, grounded not in achievement but in authenticity.

This transformation is not isolated to one individual. Across various communities, stories abound of firstborns who have embraced acceptance and witnessed profound changes in their lives. Consider the testimony of Mark, the eldest son in a family burdened by expectations of career success. Mark felt compelled to become an attorney, despite harboring a passion for the arts. He pursued a law degree, all the while battling the internal turmoil of living a life that was not his own. It wasn't until a mentor introduced him to the idea of living authentically and accepting one's unique path in Christ that real change began to manifest.

Mark learned to surrender his aspirations to God, recognizing that his identity was not found in fulfilling family expectations but rather in being a faithful steward of the gifts God had given him. This shift in perspective empowered him to pursue a career in graphic design, a field where he could express his creativity and find fulfillment. By embracing acceptance, Mark transformed his life from one of pressure and anxiety to one of joy and purpose.

Acceptance also invites a nurturing community into the process of restoration. Firstborns often feel isolated, believing they must shoulder their burdens alone. However, through authentic connection with others, they can experience the beauty of shared struggles. Embracing vulnerability in community settings helps break the chains of isolation, leading to authentic support and encouragement. This idea resonates strongly within church communities, where firstborns often discover that they are not alone in their battles. They find others who share similar stories of striving and acceptance, and they learn the value of walking alongside one another in faith.

Reflective practices play an essential role in the acceptance journey. Readers are encouraged to take time for introspection, reflecting on their personal paths to acceptance. Some questions to consider may include:

1. What are the specific expectations I feel pressure to meet as a firstborn?

2. How have these expectations impacted my self-view and faith journey?

3. In what ways do I resist surrendering my struggles to God?

4. How can I cultivate a heart of humility and trust in my relationship with Christ?

5. What steps can I take to embrace my identity as a child of God, rather than a performer?

Engaging with such questions can unlock deeper understanding and encourage proactive steps toward embracing acceptance. Reflection helps firstborns recognize that their journey of faith is unique; it is not merely about conforming to roles but about cultivating a genuine relationship with Christ.

The journey to acceptance culminates in a powerful embrace of identity, leading individuals to walk in their true worth as children of God. Acceptance signifies not merely an acknowledgment of faith but an active engagement with the redemptive powers of Christ. The crucifixion and resurrection are reminders that every struggle, every doubt, and every feeling of inadequacy is met with grace. Firstborns are invited to participate in this grace, reclaiming the narrative of their lives as one of hope and transformation.

Story after story confirms that acceptance unlocks new horizons. Consider Rachel, who spent years grappling with feelings of unworthiness tied to her firstborn status. Until she embraced acceptance, negative self-talk clouded her perception of herself. After encountering a loving community and experiencing God's grace, Rachel began to view herself through a new lens. As she absorbed scriptural truths and shared her journey with others, she shed layers of shame. Her acceptance was not just a one-time event; it became an ongoing journey where every day, she chooses to trust God with her identity.

As Rachel reflects on her transformation, she recognizes how pivotal acceptance was in reframing her story. The journey may be challenging, but it is one filled with profound moments of clarity, healing, and renewed purpose. Her testimony highlights how acceptance can replace despair with hope, leading individuals to grasp the truth that they are deeply loved and valued.

Acceptance leads to restoration—a reclaiming of what was lost through the burdens of expectation and striving. As firstborns internalize their identities in Christ, they begin to experience radical shifts within themselves. Relationships that were once strained due to the weight of perfectionism become spaces of grace, fostering deeper connections with family and community. The ripple effect of this transformation extends beyond the individual, creating a wholesome atmosphere where acceptance and love abound.

In closing, the path to acceptance is marked by humility, trust, and an unwavering belief in the transformative power of Christ. Firstborns are reminded that their identities do not have to be tethered to familial expectations or societal norms. Instead, acceptance opens the door to new possibilities, inviting them to step into their roles as beloved children of God.

Readers are encouraged to reflect on their journeys of acceptance. As they confront their struggles, lean into community, and pursue a relationship with Christ, they may find that acceptance is not merely a destination but a continual act of surrender—a powerful declaration of faith that leads to redemption and restoration. Through acceptance, firstborns can embrace a renewed sense of purpose, anchored in the love and grace of Christ, transforming their lives and the lives of those around them.

CHAPTER 14

RECLAIMING IDENTITY IN CHRIST

The journey of reclaiming identity in Christ is particularly poignant for firstborns, who often grow up with a sense of added responsibility and expectation. Society, families, and even religious circles often imbue the role of the firstborn with specific weights—be it through the inherited mantle of leadership or the undue pressure to excel. Along with these expectations comes a unique struggle, where the firstborn can find themselves tangled in a web of identity shaped more by societal demands than by God's affirming love.

To reclaim their identity, firstborns must first engage in a journey of understanding their inherent worth as children of God. This realization often starts with a shift in perspective—recognizing that their value is not derived from familial roles, achievements, or the societal definition of success but is rooted in their divine creation. In Genesis 1:27, the fundamental truth is laid bare: "So God created mankind in his own image, in the image of God he created them; male and female he created them." Understanding this scripture anchors firstborns in reality that they are not mere contributors to family legacy but are reflections of the divine.

Personal testimonies often illuminate the path of understanding and transformation. Take, for example, the story of Sarah, a firstborn who spent most of her life trying to meet her family's expectations. "From a young age, I was told that I had to set the standard for my siblings," she recalls. The weight of these expectations made her feel suffocated and anxious. "It felt like my identity was wrapped up in being perfect. I longed for my dreams, but there was always this pressure to uphold the family name.

Sarah's breakthrough began when she encountered a community that emphasized grace and acceptance. She attended a retreat focused on identity in Christ, where she had the chance to explore her worth beyond her performance. "For the first time, I realized that God loved me just as I was, imperfections and all. It was liberating," she shares. This awakening sparked a journey of self- discovery steeped in prayer and scripture, allowing her to shed the burdens of expectations and embrace her identity in Christ.

The Bible is replete with reassurances about identity and value. Romans 8:1 declares, "Therefore, there is now no condemnation for those who are in Christ Jesus." This promise serves as a gentle reminder that acceptance is rooted in belonging rather than performance. For firstborns, this grace can profoundly impact their psyche—transforming guilt and inadequacy into empowerment and freedom.

Another significant aspect of reclaiming identity is the communal support that often plays a crucial role in this journey. Firstborns can feel isolated in their struggles, believing they must bear challenges alone. However, accountability and encouragement from fellow believers can catalyze healing. Gathering with others who share similar experiences fosters a supportive environment where vulnerability is welcomed, and shared testimonies create a tapestry of understanding.

Consider the case of David, who spent years feeling responsible for his younger siblings after their parents' divorce. He absorbed the role of caretaker yet battled inner turmoil and confusion about his own identity. "I thought I had to always be the strong one. It became exhausting," he reflects. However, a close friend nudged him to join a small group focused on discussing God's love and identity. In this safe space, he began to unravel his feelings of inadequacy. "Hearing how others struggled with their own expectations made me feel less alone. We encouraged one another, and I realized I didn't have to carry this burden by myself."

Through these connections, firstborns can reclaim their identities by recognizing their shared humanity with others. The honest dialogue fosters an atmosphere of grace that enables healing, where the collective understanding of struggling with expectations becomes a stepping stone to embracing God's view of identity.

As firstborns embark on the path of reclaiming their identities, it is also essential to engage in reflective practices that affirm their worth. Journaling, for example, becomes an empowering tool in this process. Writing down personal discoveries, prayers, and affirmations can help illuminate the path to self-awareness, while scriptural readings guide firstborns in focusing on their identity in Christ.

An example is Mary, a firstborn who often felt her worth was tied to her academic achievements. She began journaling her thoughts during her quiet time with God, reflecting on her perceptions and the truth of who she was in Christ. Within weeks, she found herself writing affirmations like: "I am loved, I am accepted, and I am enough," alongside verses such as Ephesians 2:10, which states, "For we are God's handiwork, created in Christ Jesus to do good works." Over time, these practices began to reshape her inner dialogue. "Writing became a lifeline. I can now catch those negative thoughts and replace them with God's truth," she states.

Additionally, forming new habits can enhance the reclamation of identity. Firstborns can cultivate spiritual disciplines such as prayer, meditation, and serving others. Each practice serves as a reminder of their place in God's family and the identity they possess as His beloved.

Each act of service allows firstborns to engage in purposeful living, reminding them that their identities are multi-faceted. They are not merely leaders, caretakers, or overachievers; they are children of the Most High God, called to reflect His love within the world. This understanding fosters accommodation and redefinition of their roles, not as burdens to carry but as opportunities to bless others. Even the act of serving peers can encourage firstborns to see beyond the constraints placed upon them.

Consider how Lisa, a high-achieving firstborn, thrum with anxiety at each family gathering. She felt the spotlight's heat due to her educational accomplishments and struggled to balance her identity with a desire for true connection. However, she found solace in volunteering at a local shelter. The experience allowed her to witness firsthand the unconditional love and acceptance she sought. "In serving others, I found freedom. I didn't have to be the perfect daughter anymore; I could just be me," she reflects.

The clarity gained from these experiences transforms the narrative firstborns tell themselves. Embracing their identity in Christ liberates them from the chains of societal or familial expectations, granting them the ability to step into greater freedom and purpose. As they interact with other believers, they begin to discover their unique contributions to the body of Christ, further solidifying their identity as more than just firstborns but as part of a greater spiritual family. Fostering discussions within families can also assist in reclaiming each family member's identity. Parents and guardians can play an integral role in shaping how firstborns perceive themselves by affirming their worth. Consistently expressing love beyond achievements cultivates an atmosphere where acknowledging one another as God's beloved takes precedence over familial standards.

In the same breath, it is valuable for firstborns to affirm those around them, creating a culture of support. Mutual encouragement ensures that no one feels left to shoulder their identity struggles alone. Through humble frankness, discussions may lead to shared understanding and healing within family dynamics as they collectively affirm their identities in Christ.

The importance of prayer cannot be overstated in this journey of identity reclamation. Firstborns can cultivate consistent communication with God, expressing their fears, dreams, and struggles. This active dialogue nurtures trust and deepens their connection with Christ. Psalms 139:14 declares, "I praise you because I am fearfully and wonderfully made; your works are wonderful, I know that full well."

When praying through identity struggles, incorporating this verse can serve as an uplifting reminder that they are crafted for a profound purpose, utilizing their skills, personality traits, and inherent abilities. God's artistry in each life reveals that they are designed to carry His light to the world in unique ways, freeing them from the pressure to conform or compete.

In this endeavor, regular engagement with the Scriptures also proves vital as firstborns navigate their identities. Meditating on passages about God's love, grace, and intentions can solidify their beliefs and render their identities as cherished children. Implementing verses like Isaiah 43:4, "Since you are precious and honored in my sight, and because I love you, I will give people in exchange for you, nations in exchange for your life," can profoundly impact their self- perception. Such biblical truths lead firstborns not only to know but to also outwardly reflect purification as they walk in their God-given identities.

Importantly, firstborns should also realize that the journey of reclaiming identity is both ongoing and dynamic. Challenges will arise, but embracing the reality that these struggles don't define them is essential. The process involves continual recalibration, discovering and rediscovering their place in Christ through every season of life. As they reflect on and embrace their identities, the journey yields resilience built not on striving for perfection but rather on resting in God's love and acceptance.

In the grand narrative of their lives, firstborns are invited to weave their experiences and testimonies into the collective story of faith within their communities. This shared journey fosters a culture of understanding, acceptance, and love, encouraging others to rise and reclaim their identities as well. As they lift one another through shared struggles, firstborns embody a testimony of redemption that ripples across the lives of many, guiding others to find their identities rooted in Christ.

In conclusion, reclaiming identity in Christ offers firstborns an opportunity to rise above expectations, pressures, and burdens. By understanding their worth as children of God, engagingin practices that affirm theiridentities, and fostering supportive connections, they embark on a transformative journey. As pivotal voices in their families and communities, they carry the incredible responsibility of reflecting God's love and grace, anchoring their identities not in the weight of being first but in the beauty of being loved. Ultimately, as they embrace this new identity, they become warriors of light, illuminating the path for others to follow, all while standing firm in the truth of who they are—beloved children of God, chosen and cherished.

CHAPTER 15

STORIES OF RESTORATION

The sun cast a warm glow over the small gathering as firstborns shared stories that were both heart-wrenching and triumphant. In these testimonies lay the essence of redemption that no matter what challenges one faces, hope and restoration are possible through faith. Each story was a thread woven into a tapestry of extraordinary resilience, binding together the struggles and victories of the firstborns who stood before us, ready to inspire.

Michael, the eldest of four siblings, began his story with a tremor in his voice. "Growing up, I was always the responsible one, the one expected to set an example for my younger brothers and sisters. While I embraced this role, it became overwhelming. I was consumed by the need to maintain a facade of perfection, and any mistakes I made felt catastrophic." Michael paused, his eyes shimmering with unshed tears. "In my pursuit of being the perfect firstborn, I lost touch with who I truly was and what I wanted in life. I felt isolated, constantly battling the fear of letting everyone down."

He described a particularly dark period in his life, one marked by anxiety and self-doubt. "Amid my struggles, I sought relief in unhealthy habits. Instead of turning to God, I turned away, believing I had disappointed Him too deeply." His voice quavered as he recalled the low point when he realized he had lost everything: his relationships, his dreams, and even his sense of self-worth.

But it was in that darkness that Michael profoundly encountered Jesus. "A friend invited me to a church service, and it was there I felt something shift in my heart. As I listened to the message, I realized I wasn't alone. The pastor spoke about redemption and grace in a way that renewed my hope." It was a turning point, a moment when Michael allowed God to step in and heal the wounds he had tried to hide. "I began to understand that my identity wasn't tied to my achievements or failures but to who I was in Christ. That realization sparked a journey of restoration that has transformed my life." Next, Sarah shared her own story, her voice steady but filled with emotion. As a firstborn daughter, she felt weighed down by societal and familial expectations. "I always thought that my worth was measured by how well I performed. I was the straight-A student, the athlete, the role model. But as I entered adulthood, I grappled with the unbearable pressure to succeed. I felt trapped." She went on to describe her struggle with impostor syndrome, a shadow that loomed large as she pursued a career in a competitive field.

Sarah reached a breaking point during her final semester of college when the pressures of balancing her studies and her family's expectations became too much. "One night, overwhelmed and exhausted, I broke down and cried out to God. For the first time, I poured out my heart without holding back. I realized that I had been neglecting the very relationship that could strengthen me." Through prayer and reflection, Sarah started to redefine her identity beyond the expectations placed on her by others.

"I began to discover my authentic self, embracing my strengths, my weaknesses, and the unique path God was guiding me toward," she said, smiling as she recalled her journey. "Now, I find joy in the work I do, and I've let go of the fear of not being enough. My worth is anchored in Christ, and that truth sets me free."

As the group listened, a palpable sense of support filled the room. Each shared story reinforced a central theme: Restoration begins with vulnerability and honesty before God. It's a realization echoed by Rachel, who had battled feelings of inadequacy since childhood. As the eldest daughter of a single mother, she felt responsible for contributing to the household and supporting her siblings. "I thought I had to be the adult, the caretaker, and that burden became my identity," she began.

Rachel described how her sense of obligation turned into a suffocating weight. "I often neglected my own needs, convinced that appearing strong was more important than admitting I was struggling." Ultimately, the façade crumbled when she suffered a breakdown at work, leading her to seek help. "It was there, in therapy, that I learned I couldn't pour from an empty cup, no matter how hard I tried. I had to learn to care for myself, to acknowledge my own pain."

Her breakthrough moment came during a counseling session focused on spiritual identity. "The counselor said something that struck me deeply: 'Your value is not determined by what you do or how much you take on, but by the love God has for you.' That was a revelation that set me on a path toward healing. I started incorporating prayer into my daily routine and sought community support. My faith began to blossom as I surrendered my need for control."

Each individual shared personal revelations that illuminated the innate power of God's grace. Toward the end of the gathering, Mark took a deep breath, ready to share his testimony. The room fell silent as he began recounting a different struggle: addiction. "For years, I battled substance abuse, rooted in deep-seated feelings of inadequacy. I thought I was unworthy of love and acceptance, which drove me deeper into my addiction." Mark opened up about the spiral of despair that led him to homelessness and desperation.

"The turning point came during a moment of surrender in a rehabilitation center. I felt utterly broken, but I also felt God calling me back. With every tear, I poured out my heart, asking for help." Through this arduous process and with the support of a faith-based program, Mark found a faith community that embraced him despite his past. "I felt like the prodigal son returning home," he said with a smile, tears of gratitude streaming down his face.

"I learned that my past does not define me. In Christ, I'm a new creation," he affirmed. "Restoration doesn't erase the pain, but it transforms it into a testimony of God's faithfulness. I want others to understand this truth, to know that redemption is always possible."

As the stories flowed, an overwhelming sense of unity enveloped the room. The firstborns standing together ensured that no one felt alone in their struggles. Each testimony emphasized a powerful truth: Restoration through faith creates ripples of hope that extend beyond individual journeys. It fosters a community rooted in shared experiences of adversity and grace.

The gathering concluded with an open invitation for attendees to reflect on their own stories. "Each one of us carries a story of struggle and triumph," said the host. "Those stories matter. They remind us that we are not alone and that transformation through Christ is possible. We invite you to share your journey, not just as an act of vulnerability but as a call to inspire others who may be walking through similar darkness.

As participants began to share, there was a palpable sense of healing in the room. Voice after voice, stories poured forth, revealing the depths of pain and the heights of hope. Some spoke of family conflicts and the pressure to be perfect. Others shared stories of restoration after loss or failures that defined their youth. Each narrative wove a deeper understanding of the bonds shared as firstborns navigating the complexities of life.

Marissa, a young mother, spoke with conviction, detailing how she struggled to reconcile her role as a firstborn with her identity as a parent. "I wanted to be the perfect mom while carrying the weight of my family's expectations. It took me years to realize that being a parent meant demonstrating grace to my children, just as I must learn to show grace to myself. I've started involving my kids in my faith journey instead of trying to shield them from my struggles, and that has cultivated an open environment where we learn together." Her story resonated with many. The narratives created space for attendees to lean into their imperfections and embrace their authenticity. They immersed themselves in a collective atmosphere grounded in understanding and acceptance. Stories turned into soaring testimonies—not just of personal victories, but of the incredible resilience of the community they formed together.

As the night wore on, the gathering concluded with a solemn prayer, invoking a blessing of unity and healing over all firstborns. "May we continue to be brave in sharing our journeys. Let us remember that our stories not only reflect our struggles but also the light of Christ that shines within us."

With solemn resolution, the host called on each person present to encourage one another to press forward, sharing their testimonies and empowering their peers with the hope of transformation. They pledged to cultivate an environment where support, empathy, and understanding could flourish, reminding each other that despite hardships, there is always the opportunity for restoration.

Finally, as part of this gathering, a call to action was articulated for everyone to take this mission beyond this space. "We encourage you all to continue sharing your stories, whether it's in private conversations or broader community platforms. Your testimony has the power to inspire and uplift others who may feel lost," the host concluded, highlighting the strength found in vulnerability.

The stories shared that evening became interwoven with every individual's journey, creating a rich tapestry that celebrated the courage, vulnerability, and faith shared among firstborns. There was an undeniable sense that the evening extended beyond personal restoration; it proclaimed a community where every firstborn could find hope, support, and strength in their relationship with Christ. As members embraced one another and shared their final thoughts, it was a hopeful reminder that through storytelling, a collective healing could transform not just lives but hearts, drawing each person closer to the promised restoration that awaits them in faith.

CHAPTER 16

TESTIMONIES OF TRIUMPH

Personal Stories of Victory

As the sun set over the horizon, casting a golden hue on the world below, Sarah sat quietly on her porch, lost in thought. The weight of her firstborn status had followed her throughout her life, shaping her expectations, decisions, and relationships. Raised in a Christian household, she had always been aware of the familial expectations placed on her shoulders. As the eldest, she was expected to be the role model for her siblings, the one who blazed the trail of success while managing to uphold the family's reputation. But beneath that facade lay a story of relentless struggle, self-doubt, and ultimately, profound victory.

Sarah vividly recalled her early experiences of feeling inadequate. Her parents often compared her achievements with those of her friends, and though she excelled academically, she felt as if she were never enough. "You should be more like Jennifer," her father would say, a harmless yet piercing comment that lingered in her heart long after it was uttered. The constant pressure to outdo herself led to intense perfectionism, which eventually resulted in burnout during her college years.

At first, she tried to mask her feelings, burying her anxieties beneath a mountain of responsibilities. It wasn't until her second year in college that Sarah faced a crisis. She struggled to keep up with homework while juggling a part-time job and supporting her siblings. One evening, overwhelmed by fatigue and despair, Sarah found herself sitting in her car after a long day, tears streaming down her face. That was the moment she surrendered her burdens to God.

"God, I can't do this anymore," she cried out, feeling an overwhelming sense of hopelessness and exhaustion. In that moment of despair, she felt a calmness wash over her—a whisper of reassurance in the storm of her struggles. It was the beginning of her journey toward healing and empowerment.

Sarah began attending a campus Bible study group, where she met others who shared similar struggles. It was there that she learned the importance of vulnerability, and she slowly opened up about her feelings of inadequacy. Each meeting became an opportunity for her to process her emotions and turn to scripture for encouragement. It was transformative; she began to view her firstborn status not as a curse but as a unique calling—the opportunity to lead, inspire, and lift others.

As the weeks turned into months, Sarah found strength in her newfound faith. She started to embrace her identity as a beloved child of God, learning that her worth was not dependent on comparisons or academic achievements. Embracing vulnerability led to deep friendships, and she felt empowered to share her story with others. Eighteen months later, Sarah graduated with honors—this time, not seeking approval, but celebrating her journey and the freedom she found in Christ.

Her story did not end with graduation. Several years later, during a family gathering, Sarah witnessed her youngest sister struggling under the weight of expectations similar to those she had once faced. This time, with a heart of compassion, Sarah linked arms with her sister and walked her through the healing journey she herself had experienced. Together, they explored scripture, prayed, and celebrated victories—both small and large. In sharing her story, Sarah had transformed her past struggles into a source of strength and support for her siblings, breaking the cycle of comparison and pressure.

In a different part of the country, John's story spiraled into unexpected territory. As the firstborn of six, John grew up in a large family where expectations were not just high; they were extreme. His parents were immigrants seeking a better life in America, and the burdens of their dreams rested squarely on his shoulders. "You are my hope for a better future," his father would tell him. While this fueled John's determination to succeed, it also instilled an undeniable fear of failure.

John excelled academically and athletically, but in his heart, he battled spiraling insecurities. The pressure intensified when he reached his senior year of high school, and one fateful day, it crescendoed into a health scare. He collapsed during a basketball game, his body protesting the relentless pressure. Diagnosed with anxiety and exhaustion, John felt the world tremble beneath him.

Frustrated by the limitations that anxiety imposed on his life, he withdrew from the things he loved the most—sports, friends, even family. It was during this season of darkness that John encountered a mentor at his church who would change his life. This mentor, a local pastor, recognized the battle within John and guided him to a deeper understanding of faith.

"John, God doesn't want you to be perfect. He wants your heart," the pastor told him one evening as they sat under the soft glow of the church lights. Those words pierced John's heart, igniting a flicker of hope.

The journey toward recovery began that evening. John learned that vulnerability was not weakness; it was, in fact, a profound expression of faith. Over time, he began to share his struggles openly with his family and friends, which helped dismantle the unrealistic expectations he had carried. Instead of being paralyzed by fear, John embraced counseling, meditation, and prayer as vital tools for managing his anxiety.

From those depths, victory rose—a journey marked not by the absence of struggles, but by the presence of faith and community. With newfound clarity, John joined a local basketball league, not as the sole hope for his family, but as a teammate intent on fostering support within the game. He became a leader, not just through success but through shared experiences and encouragement.

Now an advocate for mental health awareness, John's voice echoes a message of resilience. He shares his journey across communities and schools, fostering understanding about the pressures faced by firstborns and the importance of mental health. Each testimony he shares serves as a beacon of hope for those who feel trapped by expectations.

As the pages of life turned, Maria's story unfolded under different circumstances. As a Latina firstborn in an immigrant family, Maria often felt torn between two worlds. The expectations from her parents—who expected her to be responsible and help at home—conflicted starkly with the pressures from her peers, who encouraged her to embrace a more carefree adolescent lifestyle.

During her high school years, Maria made the bold decision to pursue the arts, specifically dance. It was a passion that brought her immense joy, yet the fear of disappointing her parents loomed heavily over her. Torn between her dreams and familial obligations, she pushed herself to the limits, often sacrificing her own happiness for the sake of fulfilling others' expectations.

The breaking point came when Maria received a scholarship for a prestigious dance program. Her parents, hesitant to support the path of "impractical" choices, urged her to reconsider. The pressure mounted, leading to heated discussions at home, and once again, Maria felt her identity unscrewed and fractured. She stood at a crossroads, wondering if she should relinquish her dreams for the sake of her family's approval.

Amid her turmoil, Maria sought solace in prayer. One evening, feeling particularly disheartened, she flipped open her Bible and landed on a passage in Jeremiah: "For I know the plans I have for you, declares the Lord..." (Jeremiah 29:11). In that moment, her heart ignited with hope, and she felt the call to pursue her dreams wholeheartedly.

With a newfound courage, Maria approached her parents to express her desires earnestly. She explained the importance of pursuing her passion for dance as a means of honoring the sacrifices they made for her. To her surprise, they listened; the conversation opened the door to dialogue, understanding, and ultimately support.

As Maria followed her dreams, she began to flourish in her art. Passion ignited a sense of purpose within her, allowing her position as the firstborn to transform from a burden to an opportunity for leadership. She initiated dance workshops in her community, wanting to give back to younger girls who shared her struggles. By sharing her journey, Maria empowered others, showing them that dreams should not be sacrificed at the altar of expectations.

Meanwhile, across states, Justin's life was also a poignant testament to the resilience of firstborns. As a young man growing up in a wealthy family, expectations came dressed in a different ensemble. The pressure to succeed manifested as a gilded cage, suffocating him. Each achievement felt hollow, often overshadowed by comparisons made by his parents to their wealthy friends' children.

In college, Justin enrolled in a prestigious business program but soon felt the pang of dissatisfaction. Despite earning top marks, he dreaded the future his parents envisioned for him—a life of corporate success that left little room for his creative pursuits. The pressure reached a peak during his junior year, leading to an identity crisis that prompted him to question everything he had known.

One fateful evening, while walking home from class, he stumbled upon an impromptu art show showcasing student artwork. Captivated by the raw expression of creativity and emotion, Justin felt an awakening. It sparked a desire he had long buried—the urge to pursue art. That night, he made a radical decision: he would shift his academic focus to the arts, a choice that felt both terrifying and exhilarating.

Justin bravely shared his decision with his family during dinner. The initial reaction was one of disbelief and disappointment; they could not fathom a life outside of their carefully laid plans. But through his unwavering conviction and heartfelt expression, Justin slowly unraveled the fears that held him back and maintained a firm belief that it was possible to reconcile passion and purpose.

The journey ahead was fraught with challenges and uncertainties. Yet through faith, he embraced the resistance he encountered. He began to showcase his artwork at local galleries, bridging the gap between his passion and potential. For Justin, victory was not merely stepping into a career—it was a reclaiming of his identity.

Seeking to empower those who faced similar struggles, Justin launched workshops for firstborns battling familial expectations. He created safe spaces where participants could share their journeys, rediscover their passions, and reclaim their identities. Each workshop became a haven of vulnerability and strength, uniting a community in the pursuit of authenticity.

Each of these narratives weaves a tapestry of struggles faced by firstborns, but they also share threads of victory—a celebration not solely of personal achievement, but rather the transformative power of faith, community, and self-acceptance. The journeys of Sarah, John, Maria, and Justin may differ in context, but they converge in one shared space: the realization that victory often emerges from trials and tribulations.

As readers engage with these stories, they are invited to reflect upon their own journeys. Triumph is not merely a destination; it is often a messy road filled with overcoming fears, embracing faith, and leaning into community. Perhaps within these testimonies, firstborns will find an inspirational reminder that they are not alone in their struggles and that their stories hold the potential for profound impact.

The victories shared within this subchapter highlight the pivotal role faith plays in breaking chains that bind firstborns to the heavy weight of expectations. With each story, there exists an echo of hope, a reminder that through faith and community, firstborns are equipped to transform their struggles into testimonies of triumph. As Sarah, John, Maria, and Justin confidently walk their paths, may they inspire readers to do the same, embracing vulnerability, stepping into identity, and pursuing victory in their narratives.

CHAPTER 17

COMMUNITY IMPACT STORIES

In the lives of firstborns, where the weight of expectations often bears down heavily, community plays a pivotal role in shaping their journeys. The societal imprints on firstborns—burdened with responsibilities and aspirations—can be softened through the support and encouragement found within the fabric of community. This subchapter seeks to illuminate the stories of firstborns who have navigated their unique struggles with the unwavering support of those around them. Through shared experiences and testimonies, we will uncover how relationships and mentorship within their communities have not only aided in personal growth but also strengthened their spiritual foundations.

As we delve into the profound impact of community, we find that many firstborns have faced similar challenges, whether it be living under the shadow of high expectations, managing family dynamics that can sometimes breed envy and competition, or feeling like they must bear the burdens of their families. Each story discussed in this subchapter serves as a testament to the idea that no firstborn's journey is ever truly solitary.

Consider Emily, a vibrant firstborn who felt suffocated by the expectations placed upon her by her family. From a young age, she excelled academically and was often characterized as "the responsible one." Emily was expected not only to excel but to also guide her younger siblings. This immense pressure led to feelings of isolation and anxiety, as she struggled to reconcile her aspirations with the reality of her responsibilities. However, Emily found solace in her church community, where she encountered her mentor, Sarah, an inspiring woman who had once walked a similar path.

Sarah's journey had been fraught with challenges as well, and she was genuinely passionate about empowering young women in her community. Recognizing Emily's potential, Sarah took the time to invest in her life, offering not just guidance but also friendship. Through regular mentoring sessions that included prayer, counseling, and honest conversations, Emily began to see herself through a different lens. With Sarah's support, she learned to set boundaries regarding her responsibilities while also pursuing her passions.

Inspired by the thriving relationship she found in her mentorship with Sarah, Emily began volunteering in the youth ministry at her church, encouraging other firstborns grappling with similar pressures. As she shared her own struggles and triumphs, Emily created a ripple effect within her community, fostering an atmosphere of openness where others felt empowered to share their own stories. It was in this environment of shared vulnerability that Emily truly flourished. Her mentoring experience exemplifies the powerful relational dynamic that can exist within a community. The realization dawned upon herthatshe was not merelya firstborn carryingtheheavymantle of expectations but a leader capable of inspiring others. Through community support, her faith deepened, and she recognized her worth beyond societal expectations; she was a daughter of the King, deserving of grace, love, and a life that goes beyond mere duty.

Then there's Mark, a firstborn son who grew up in a household that valued achievement above all else. His parents, with their relentless focus on academic and athletic success, set the standard to an impossible height. Mark, feeling the heat of constant comparison, often found himself battling feelings of inadequacy. However, during his college years, he discovered a group of firstborns who gathered once a week to support one another in their unique journeys. This community was comprised of individuals from diverse backgrounds but shared common firstborn experiences.

These gatherings became a lifeline for Mark. He learned that others too struggled with the weight of expectations and the fear of failure. Through shared stories, they helped one another navigate the tumultuous waters of self-doubt. Mark found himself not only listened to but also uplifted by the encouragement of his peers. As he openly discussed his challenges, he discovered that vulnerability could birth strength.

One of Mark's most significant revelations occurred when they began discussing the importance of balancing personal ambition with a sense of spiritual fulfillment. With the guidance of one of the group leaders, a trusted teacher, they initiated a prayer structure where members shared their dreams, not just for academic or career achievements but for their spiritual journeys. Mark realized he had been so focused on measuring his worth through success that he had neglected his spiritual walk with God. With the support of his community, he began redirecting his focus, leading to remarkable spiritual growth.

The stories of Emily and Mark underscore an essential truth: community creates spaces for healing and empowerment. These spaces are not only vital for personal gratification but also serve to strengthen one's sense of faith. They illustrate the transformative power of shared experiences as firstborns find safety and support amid their daily trials.

As we explore the essence of community further, we must also consider the pivotal roles of mentorship and encouragement. Take a moment to reflect on Clara, another firstborn whose life narrative reflects the significance of community engagement. Clara grew up in a community where mentorship was deeply ingrained in their culture. During her formative years, she was paired with a mentor, Mrs. Thompson, who was a revered elder in her neighborhood.

Mrs. Thompson not only imparted wisdom but served as a stalwart presence throughout Clara's youth, anchoring her amidst storms of self-doubt and familial expectations. The two engaged in monthly meetings wherein Clara shared her dreams, aspirations, and fears. Mrs. Thompson's mentorship evolved into a beautiful friendship marked by genuine respect, encouragement, and shared faith. This enriching relationship equipped Clara with the tools to thrive both academically and spiritually.

With the unwavering support of her mentor, Clara began to engage with younger members of her community, mentoring them as Mrs. Thompson had done for her. She created workshops focused on building confidence, spiritual growth, and academic success, where participants learned from her firsthand experiences as a firstborn.

Clara discovered that leading others brought an intrinsic satisfaction, allowing her to embrace her identity in Christ, recognizing that her triumphs could foster collective growth.

This cyclical nature of mentorship is crucial; Clara's successes became a beacon of hope for others, perpetuating the cycle of support within the community. The emotional bond formed through these interactions reflects the kingdom's principle of empowering one another—a beautiful tapestry woven through love, support, and faith.

The theme of community also emerges powerfully in the church setting, where congregations serve as sanctuaries for firstborns learning to navigate their identities. For many young people, the church becomes an essential support system. David, a firstborn navigating his late teenage years, particularly embraced this concept. Initially reluctant to join the youth group because of a perceived divergence from his personal identity, David eventually found himself welcomed into a community that resonated with his struggles.

One evening at a youth retreat, David met others who shared his burdens—the feeling of inadequacy, the pressure of responsibility, and the desire to please others. In a session dedicated to personal testimony, he opened about his challenges, pouring out the weight he had carried in silence for so long. The hearts of his peers resonated with him; they prayed for him, shared their own experiences of struggle, and offered words of encouragement that felt like a warm embrace.

This experience catalyzed David's transformation. He began to realize that vulnerability was not a sign of weakness but an avenue for authentic connection. As he engaged more deeply with his youth group, David emerged as a supportive figure in his community, mentoring others who faced similar internal battles.

David's story reflects a vital message: the power of community is amplified when individuals contribute actively to it. His shift from feeling isolated to being a supportive figure for others illustrates the enriching cycle of support that can be cultivated among firstborns, allowing them to transcend struggles and embrace their roles within the body of Christ.

Even amidst challenges, the role of community cannot be overstated. Each story tells a tale of personal and collective triumph—proof that through fellowship and faith, individuals can rise above struggles. They serve as reminders that communities are designed to function not just as a social network, but as systems of support, encouragement, and empowerment.

As we reflect on the importance of community, it invites us to consider our own support systems. Who are the mentors in our lives? Are we actively engaging with peers who uplift and inspire us? The stories featured here encourage readers to seek out and nurture relationships with those who understand the journey of a firstborn. By engaging within their communities, firstborns can discover the beautiful truth that they are not alone in their struggles. We also realize that strength is often found in the act of giving. Just as Emily, Mark, Clara, and David leaned on others, they also made the conscious choice to pour into the lives of those around them. This reciprocity fosters a sense of belonging and connection that transcends mere friendship; it cultivates a community rooted in shared encounters and a collective journey through faith.

In conclusion, the stories shared throughout this subchapter exemplify how firstborns have experienced triumph through the loving embrace of community. In moments where personal struggles may have threatened to overshadow their identities, these individuals illuminated pathways toward hope, healing, and spiritual growth by forging connections with others. Each narrative serves as encouragement to rise with one another, breaking the constraints of isolation to bask in the beauty of shared experiences.

Ultimately, by fostering relationships grounded in love and support, firstborns can redefine their roles, embracing the promise of a rich community cultivated in faith. The strength discovered within these connections enables individuals to not only navigate their personal journeys but also impact the lives of others with grace, resilience, and purpose. As you read these testimonies of triumph, may you be inspired to seek out and invest in your own communities, stepping boldly into the collective narrative that shapes us all.

The fulfilling journey of the firstborn is profoundly intertwined with the relationships we cultivate, reminding us of the truth that we are better together.

CHAPTER 18

LESSONS LEARNED AND SHARED WISDOM

Throughout the testimonies shared in this chapter, a rich tapestry of experiences from firstborns has emerged, illustrating the profound impact of their journeys through struggles, victories, and transformations. The stories reflect not only personal trials but also a collective narrative that underscores crucial lessons learned along the way. These lessons resonate deeply, offering insight into resilience, faith, and the significance of community. As we distill these stories, it becomes evident that firstborns carry a unique weight, one that encompasses expectations, challenges, and the potential for remarkable growth.

Resilience, a core theme woven throughout these testimonies, serves as a powerful reminder of the human spirit's capacity to endure and overcome. Many firstborns recounted moments of feeling overwhelmed by their responsibilities, often placed upon them by family dynamics and societal pressures. Yet, within these stories lay profound examples of how adversity can forge strength. For instance, in the testimony of Sarah, a firstborn who faced the burden of supporting her family's expectations, her journey from anxiety to empowerment is a testament to resilience. She learned that challenges can serve as catalysts for personal growth; through introspection and courage, she was able to redefine her narrative and emerge with a stronger sense of self.

Faith emerges as another foundational lesson from the testimonies, illuminating the role that belief in God plays in navigating life's obstacles. Several individuals recounted moments where their faith was tested, leading to a deeper understanding of God's presence and provision. Lucas, who once struggled with feelings of inadequacy, shared how his moments of doubt transformed into a renewed trust in God's plan. He learned that even during the darkest times, a faith anchored in hope can illuminate the path forward. The power of faith is not merely in its ability to provide comfort but in its capacity to inspire action and determination. This lesson encourages readers to explore their own faith journeys, recognizing the strength that comes from reliance on a higher purpose.

Community emerged as a vital thread connecting the stories of triumph. Many firstborns spoke of the importance of surrounding themselves with supportive individuals who uplift and encourage them. The testimony of Aisha illustrates this beautifully. Faced with the pressure of familial expectations, she found solace in a close- knit group of friends who understood her struggles. Through shared experiences and mutual support, Aisha realized that she did not have to bear her burdens alone. This transformative lesson emphasizes that community is not simply a backdrop to individual stories; it is a vital part of the healing and empowerment process. Readers are encouraged to examine their own networks and consider how they can both seek support and offer it to others in their communities. As we reflect on these lessons, it is essential to recognize the transformative power of sharing experiences.

Each testimony contributes a unique perspective, creating a collective narrative that celebrates triumph over adversity. Firstborns, by virtue of their roles, often become leaders not only within their families but also in their broader circles. The lessons distilled from their journeys serve as guideposts for others navigating similar paths.

Resilience teaches us that struggles are an inherent part of life, not barriers to success. It is through facing and overcoming these challenges that individuals can grow stronger and discover their true selves. Faith, meanwhile, serves as an anchor, providing a sense of purpose and direction amid chaos. For firstborns, understanding that their worth is defined not by their achievements but by their identity as children of God can lead to profound shifts in mindset. Lastly, the emphasis on community underscores the importance of connection.

Reaching out, forming friendships, and building networks of support can create an environment where everyone thrives, fostering a sense of belonging and shared purpose.

The power of shared wisdom encourages introspection; readers are invited to reflect on their own lives and consider how they can apply these lessons. What does resilience look like in their journeys? How can they cultivate deeper faith and trust in God? In what ways can they engage with their communities to both seek support and provide assistance to others? These questions serve as starting points for personal exploration, guiding readers toward actionable steps that enhance their spiritual and emotional well-being.

The shared wisdom within these testimonies extends beyond individual experiences; it calls for a collective action among firstborns. By embracing vulnerability and sharing struggles, firstborns can create an atmosphere of authenticity, fostering deeper connections within their communities. In actively participating in the collective story of firstborns, individuals can uplift one another, creating a ripple effect that empowers others to engage with their own struggles.

This subchapter serves not only as a summary of the powerful experiences shared throughout the chapter but also as a bridge to the next section of the book. As we explore the implications of living in victory, the lessons of resilience, faith, and community will continue to serve as guiding principles. Empowerment is not merely an abstract concept; it is a tangible reality that can be lived out through the choices we make each day.

By embodying the lessons learned from shared experiences, firstborns can cultivate their unique identities, embracing their roles with newfound confidence. The stories of struggle, growth, and triumph become catalysts for transformation—not only for themselves but for those around them. As readers move to the next chapter, may they carry these insights with them, continuing to seek empowerment and actively contribute to community-building among firstborns.

In conclusion, the journeys of firstborns signify more than individual triumphs; they represent the potential to inspire others, create change, and foster unity. Together, through resilience, faith, and the strength found in community, firstborns can navigate the complexities of life and emerge victorious. The lessons learned from these testimonies illuminate a path toward greater purpose and fulfillment, inviting readers to step into their identities as agents of change within their families and communities. As the narrative progresses, may it inspire a continuing commitment to growth, connection, and the shared mission of uplifting one another along the way.

CHAPTER 19

BREAKING GENERATIONAL CURSES

Understanding Generational Patterns

The concept of generational curses is one that resonates deeply within many families and cultures. Often, these patterns of sin and struggle are passed from one generation to the next, silently shaping behaviors, attitudes, and outcomes in ways that are not always immediately recognizable. For firstborns, the weight of these generational patterns can feel particularly heavy, as they often find themselves in roles that demand higher expectations and responsibilities. This subchapter seeks to unravel the complexities of generational curses, providing insights into how they manifest, especially in the lives of firstborns.

Generational curses are not merely abstract concepts; they are lived experiences. The Bible provides numerous examples that illustrate how the choices and sins of one generation can reverberate through subsequent generations. Consider the story of Abraham, Isaac, and Jacob. Each of these patriarchs made choices that not only affected their direct descendants but also shaped the nation of Israel. Abraham's deception about Sarah being his sister, for instance, was mirrored by Isaac when he, too, deceived others about Rebekah. This pattern of deception created an atmosphere of distrust within the family. Subsequently, Jacob's own lineage was marked by familial strife and conflict, characterized by deception among siblings.

These biblical narratives serve to remind us that generational patterns can compound over time, creating cycles of behavior that are challenging to break. The struggles faced by firstborns often reflect these historical echoes. In families where the firstborn is held to disproportionately high standards—whether in academic achievements, careersuccesses, or spiritualleadership—the pressure can be immense. The emotional weight of these expectations can lead to feelings of inadequacy, anxiety, and, in some cases, rebellion. Many firstborns may find themselves wrestling with the sins and shortcomings of previous generations while simultaneously trying to forge their own identities.

It is essential to recognize the emotional toll that generational curses exact on firstborns. When a firstborn experiences a sense of being trapped by the failures of their predecessors, it can ignite a cycle of shame and guilt. These emotions can manifest in a variety of ways, including perfectionism, anxiety, and even anger. The expectation to "do better" than their predecessors often leaves little room for vulnerability or failure, creating an internal dialogue that is both critical and self-defeating. This dialogue can perpetuate the generational curse, as the firstborn may inadvertently pass these expectations onto the next generation.

One particular story that encapsulates this struggle comes from a firstborn whose family had a long history of patriarchs who were successful, hard-working, and respected in their communities. From an early age, he was taught that he needed to be the best at everything he attempted. His parents frequently recounted stories of their own siblings who had fallen short, emphasizing the importance of upholding the family name. As he moved into adulthood, this pressure translated into a driving need to excel in his career. However, the stress of constant comparison led to burnout and dissatisfaction, which affected his relationships and spiritual life. This firstborn's story is not unique; many individuals find themselves grappling with the weight of generational expectations. Often, these burdens manifest as anxiety or perfectionism, creating a fear of failure that looms ever larger. The biblical concept of sin and its generational impact can further complicate matters, as individuals may feel bound by unconfessed sin or unresolved issues from previous generations.

In examining generational curses, it is crucial to acknowledge that these patterns can be spiritually influenced. In the same way that family legacies can shape behaviors and attitudes, spiritual forces can also play a role. Ephesians 6:12 reminds us that our struggles are not against flesh and blood but against spiritual forces of evil. This underscores the importance of recognizing that some generational patterns may have roots in spiritual bondage, making it even more essential to confront and address these issues head-on.

The recognition of generational patterns brings with it a sense of responsibility. This responsibility requires firstborns to become aware of the tendencies, behaviors, and emotional patterns that have been passed down to them. It calls them to examine their family histories, identifying the ways in which those before them have shaped their own lives. This examination is not solely about assigning blame; rather, it is an invitation to confront the past with courage and honesty.

For many, the journey of confronting generational patterns begins with prayer and reflection. Scripture encourages followers of Christ to pray for selfish ambitions and unhealthy patterns to be revealed and relinquished. Acknowledging one's family history in prayer can serve as the first step in breaking the cycle of generational curses. During this time of seeking, individuals may recognize attitudes of fear, resentment, or inadequacy that have shaped their lives. Understanding these attitudes lays a foundation for healing and restoration.

At this juncture, it is helpful to integrate personal stories to further illuminate the theme of breaking generational patterns. Consider the story of a woman named Sarah, who was the firstborn in her family of three. Growing up, her family dynamics revolved around her mother's struggles with depression and her father's tendency to emotionally distance himself from family issues. As the eldest, Sarah felt responsible for her siblings, attempting to keep the peace and fill the emotional void left by her parents. Over time, she developed a need to be the "strong one," mirroring her parents' avoidance of emotional expression.

Throughout her adult years, Sarah noticed that this pattern continued in her relationships. She found herself unconsciously attracting emotionally unavailable partners, and she would often sacrifice her own needs to maintain harmony. In therapy, she began to recognize the weight of generational patterns, realizing that her desire to be emotionally stoic stemmed from her upbringing. Sarah's journey to confront these patterns ultimately led her to seek healing through community and therapy. She learned to express emotions and set boundaries, breaking free from the cycle of dysfunction that had permeated her family.

The importance of community support cannot be overstated in this journey. Family dynamics and generational patterns are often woven tightly into the fabric of community life. When firstborns begin the work of uncovering and confronting these issues, they should do so with the support of a trusted community—be it friends, mentors, or a faith-based group. It is within these spaces that individuals can share their experiences and learn from one another, helping to break down the barriers that generational curses impose.

Scripture supports the call to communal healing. Hebrews 10:24-25 encourages believers to stir one another up to love and good works, not forsaking assembling. This communal aspect is vital, as it fosters accountability and support, allowing individuals to share their burdens and grow together in faith. The shared journey of recognizing and breaking generational patterns can transform not only individual lives but also the broader community.

As firstborns begin to confront generational curses, they need to cultivate a mindset focused on healing and redemption. Rather than succumbing to feelings of hopelessness, they should embrace the truth found in Christ's redemptive work. Galatians 5:1 proclaims that "it is for freedom that Christ has set us free." This freedom allows firstborns to break the chains of generational patterns that have held them back and to step into a new identity rooted in Christ. To initiate this transformation, firstborns can engage in intentional practices that foster healing. Journaling can be a valuable tool for reflecting on personal experiences, unraveling feelings, and exploring family dynamics. As individuals write down their stories, they may discover patterns and tendencies that were previously obscured. This self-reflection can facilitate deeper understanding and create pathways for healing.

Additionally, incorporating prayer into daily routines can help reinforce the commitment to break free from generational curses. Asking God to reveal areas in need of healing and seeking His guidance for overcoming negative patterns can deepen one's spiritual walk. Scripture emphasizes the power of prayer in James 5:16, stating, "The prayer of a righteous person is powerful and effective." This verse serves as a reminder that spiritual engagement is integral in the journey toward breaking generational curses.

Learning to forgive is another crucial component in the process of healing. Firstborns should consider whether they need to forgive those in their family tree who may have perpetuated harmful patterns, as well as forgiving themselves for struggling with similar behaviors. Forgiveness is not about condoning or excusing past actions; rather, it is an act of obedience and freedom. Matthew 6:14-15 reminds us that if we forgive others, our heavenly Father will also forgive us. Through forgiveness, individuals can release the emotional weight of generational curses and begin to move forward in grace.

As these practices take root, firstborns may begin to witness a transformation in their lives. Breaking generational curses does not happen overnight; it is a gradual process that requires diligence and patience. The road to healing may involve stumbling and setbacks, but faith and consistent effort can lead to profound change.

In summary, understanding the generational patterns that afflict firstborns is a crucial step toward breaking the cycle of generational curses. The narratives found in Scripture provide powerful lessons that remind us of the lasting impact of choices made by previous generations. By recognizing these patterns, firstborns can begin the journey of confronting their family histories with courage, seeking healing through prayer, community, and forgiveness. As they embrace their identities rooted in Christ, they can break free from the burdens of past generations, paving the way for future generations to experience the fullness of life in Christ. In this journey of restoration, they become participants in the redemptive story of their families, bringing hope and healing to those who come after them.

CHAPTER 20

STEPS TO BREAKING FREE

The journey to breaking free from generational curses can often feel overwhelming, especially for firstborns who may carry the weight of expectations, burdens, and inherited struggles. However, there is a pathway to healing and restoration that can transform lives and break the cycle of negativity. This subchapter will outline practical steps that firstborns can take to break free from negative generational patterns, supported by the power of confession, repentance, prayer, and community. Through personal testimonies, we will illustrate the hope and transformation that is possible when one actively seeks to break free from their past.

Understanding the impact of generational curses is essential for any firstborn seeking change. These curses often manifest in repeated patterns of behavior, attitudes, and emotional struggles that can trace back through family lines. They may appear as unresolved conflict, addiction, mental health challenges, or feelings of inadequacy. Acknowledging their presence is the first step toward freedom. By recognizing how these patterns affect their lives, firstborns can begin to confront their past rather than allow it to define their future.

The first practical step in this process is confession. Confession serves as a powerful tool for breaking generational curses. When firstborns confess the specific negatives that have impacted their lives, they bring these hidden shadows into the light. This act of vulnerability can be incredibly freeing, as it allows individuals to acknowledge their struggles without fear of judgment or rejection. Confession also includes recognizing the collective nature of these struggles—understanding that they are a part of a larger familial narrative can instill a sense of solidarity in one's journey.

For example, consider the story of Sarah, a firstborn who struggled with feelings of inadequacy and the need for perfection. Growing up in a household where accomplishments were prioritized, Sarah often felt that her worth hinged on her performance. After recognizing this pattern and confessing her struggles to a trusted friend, Sarah found relief. She learned that her feelings were not unique and that many in her family shared similar burdens. By expressing her struggles, she was able to take the first crucial step toward breaking this generational pattern.

Alongside confession is the essential step of repentance. While confession requires acknowledgment of the problematic behavior and patterns, repentance takes the process a step further; it calls for a change of heart and direction. This step is crucial, as it signifies a commitment to do things differently moving forward. Repentance involves a heartfelt desire to turn away from the patterns that have enslaved generations and to pursue a new path—one rooted in faith, hope, and the transformative love of Christ.

In the same vein, another firstborn, Michael, experienced a significant shift after he repented from harboring resentment toward his parents for their unresolved issues. He recognized that carrying those grievances was not only holding him back but perpetuating a cycle of bitterness in his own life. By choosing to forgive, he released the anger and embraced a spirit of grace, thus breaking free from the emotional stronghold that had haunted his family for years.

Prayer is another essential component in the journey of breaking generational curses. It acts as both a source of strength and a means of communication with God. Firstborns are encouraged to bring their burdens before God, seeking His guidance, healing, and strength. Prayer can serve as a powerful tool to dismantle the strongholds of fear, anxiety, and doubt that often accompany generational curses. Each prayer offered is an act of faith that reaffirms one's commitment to healing and restoration.

For instance, Anna, a firstborn whose family had battled mental health challenges for generations, found solace in prayer. She made it a daily practice to surrender her fears and anxieties to God. Over time, she began to experience a sense of peace that she had not known before and felt empowered to seek therapy—a step that was crucial for her healing journey. Through prayer, Anna connected with God's promise of healing and restoration, giving her the courage to confront her family's history with mental health.

Community support is equally vital in the journey of breaking free from generational patterns. Often, firstborns shoulder the weight of familial expectations alone, feeling isolated in their struggles. However, engaging with a supportive community can foster accountability, encouragement, and healing. Through the love and guidance of others, firstborns can feel bolstered in their commitment to change. These community connections can come in various forms—friends, church groups, or family members who share similar goals.

Mark's story exemplifies the transformative power of community support. A firstborn dealing with addiction, Mark turned to a community group focused on recovery. In this setting, he discovered not only resources for overcoming his struggle but also companionship among those who understood his challenges. Through shared experiences and collective encouragement, Mark found the strength to confront his past, support others, and ultimately break free from the generational patterns that had plagued his family for years.

As firstborns gather their confessions and seek repentance, it's important to incorporate practical strategies into their daily lives. Creating a consistent routine of prayer, reflection, and connection with others can foster a supportive environment for growth. Here are some actionable steps that can help firstborns on their journey of breaking generational curses:

1. Journaling: Start a journal focused on your experiences and feelings about your place in the family. Write down patterns you recognize, specific burdens you feel, and the impacts of these on your life. This process can be cathartic and allows you to document your journey toward healing.

2. Engage in Regular Confession: Set aside time to confess your struggles either privately in prayer or to trusted confidants. The regular act of confession can help nurture a healthy relationship with your past.

3. Establish a Prayer Routine: Design a prayer schedule that suits you. Whether it's morning, evening, or throughout the day, make it a priority to connect with God regularly. If possible, join group prayer meetings to reinforce accountability.

4. Seek Professional Help: Consider therapy or counseling as a means of addressing deep-rooted emotions and behaviors stemming from generational curses. A professional can provide valuable strategies for coping and healing.

5. Find Community: Look for community groups or church gatherings where you can share your experiences and gain support. A sense of belonging can enhance your journey and provide a network of encouragement.

6. Practice Forgiveness: Make a conscious effort to forgive those in your family, including yourself. This might involve writing a letter to a family member expressing your feelings or even seeking a direct conversation.

7. Develop Healthy Relationships: Surround yourself with individuals who uplift and inspire you. Healthy friendships can provide the emotional support necessary for transformation.

8. Reflect on Progress: At regular intervals, reflect on your journey. Acknowledge the changes you have made and celebrate the victories, no matter how small. This process reinforces your commitment to healing.

Through these steps, firstborns can find empowerment in their journey toward breaking free from generational curses. It's important to remember that this is not an overnight process; rather, it is a gradual journey filled with trials, growth, and ultimately, transformation.

The testimony of Leah exemplifies the power of embracing these practical steps. As a firstborn hailing from a family afflicted by extreme anxiety and fear, Leah hesitated to share her struggle. However, after beginning to journal, pray, and engage with a local church group focused on healing, she realized she was not alone in her experience. Over time, through prayer and the support of her newfound community, Leah confronted and dismantled the fears that had long dominated her family line.

The encouragement she found in community, combined with her steps toward confession and repentance, helped her embrace her identity as a child of God. Now, Leah actively supports others who share similar anxieties, encouraging them to pursue the freedom she found. Her transformation not only liberated her but also sparked hope in those around her.

The journey of breaking free from generational curses is a sacred and transformative endeavor. It requires courage, determination, and a willingness to face the past while moving toward a hopeful future. Through confession, repentance, prayer, and the support of a fellowship, firstborns can reclaim their identities and break the cycle of negativity that may have been passed down through generations. By integrating these practical steps into their daily lives, firstborns can not only initiate their own healing but also contribute to the healing of their families and communities. As the journey unfolds, let them remember that they are never alone. Through Christ's redemptive work, they are empowered to break free from generational patterns and embrace the fullness of life that God promises. Hope awaits them, guiding them into a future unbounded by the difficulties of the past.

May firstborns emerge from this process not only as victors over their struggles but also as beacons of hope for those yet to begin their own journeys. By stepping into their new identities and living in the freedom provided by faith, they can create a legacy of healing that reverberates throughout generations to come. In doing so, they will illustrate the profound truth that, while the past may shape their experiences, it does not have to define their ultimate destiny.

CHAPTER 21

THE ROLE OF FAITH IN BREAKING CURSES

Generational curses often linger like shadows across family histories, casting a pall over the lives of individuals born into such circumstances. These patterns of pain, sin, and hardship can feel insurmountable, especially for firstborns who may bear the brunt of familial expectations and inherited struggles. However, amidst this weight, faith stands as a powerful tool for breaking these chains and ushering in renewal and transformation.

To understand how faith plays a crucial role in breaking generational curses, we must first acknowledge the biblical framework for curses and blessings. The Scriptures articulate that sin has consequences, often impacting not just the individual, but extending through familial lines. In Exodus 34:7, God declares that He "will not leave the guilty unpunished; He punishes the children and their children for the sin of the parents to the third and fourth generation." This stark warning can feel daunting, as it highlights a reality where the struggles of one generation can spill over into the next, creating a cycle that seems unbreakable. Yet, while the acknowledgment of this pattern is important, it is equally critical to focus on the transformative power of faith.

Faith in Christ serves as the ultimate antidote to the generational curse, offering redemption and a pathway to reclaim our identities and destinies. Galatians 3:13-14 beautifully encapsulates this notion: "Christ redeemed us from the curse of the law by becoming a curse for us... so that by faith we might receive the promise of the Spirit." Importantly, through our faith in Jesus, we are not only freed from the historical consequences of our families' sins but are also set on a new trajectory that aligns with

God's original intent for us. This promise of liberation beckons us to embrace our faith fully, as an active choice to trust in God's love and transformative power.

The journey of breaking generational curses often begins with the acknowledgment of the struggles we inherit. This may involve facing uncomfortable truths about our family histories and the patterns that have emerged. For many firstborns, this process can be fraught with emotion, as expectations and familial roles weigh heavily on their shoulders. It is not uncommon for firstborns to internalize the burdens of their families, feeling an intense responsibility to rectify past mistakes or to live up to the highs and lows of their relatives. In confronting these inherited challenges, faith becomes a beacon of hope—a comforting presence that assures individuals that they are not bound by their environments or histories.

A poignant example of this is found in the story of the biblical character Joseph. Despite being the favored son of Jacob, Joseph faced tremendous trials, including betrayal by his own brothers, enslavement in Egypt, and false accusations. Yet, throughout these hardships, Joseph maintained his faith in God, which ultimately allowed him to break not only personal curses but also bring about blessing to the very family that wronged him. When a famine struck, Joseph was positioned to save his family, showing that through faith, cyclical patterns of pain can be transformed into avenues of healing and restoration. This narrative articulates a crucial truth: that faith allows us to reframe our perspectives, viewing our past not as a limitation but as part of the unique tapestry through which God can work.

In practical terms, breaking generational curses through faith involves active participation in spiritual disciplines. Prayer, for instance, lays the groundwork for conversations with God and invites His intervention into our familial histories. Acknowledging the past, asking for forgiveness, and seeking God's restoration are powerful components of prayer that can set firstborns—and indeed anyone—on a path of healing.

Consider the transformative potential for a firstborn who regularly engages in prayer, specifically praying for their family lineage. They could intercede for the cessation of harmful patterns while simultaneously inviting God's presence into their family dynamics. In doing so, they can break the curse of negativity and replace it with a blessing of hope, joy, and peace. By channeling their faith through prayer, they actively participate in God's redemptive work, both in their lives and in their families.

Beyond prayer, scriptural meditation also plays a vital role in the process. The Bible contains numerous passages promising freedom from curses when we align ourselves with God. For firstborns, embracing scriptures such as 2 Corinthians 5:17—"Therefore, if anyone is in Christ, he is a new creation. The old has passed away; behold, the new has come!"—can provide reassurance and a renewed sense of identity. Engaging with these truths not only fortifies one's faith but also reinforces the idea that they are recipients of God's grace and are empowered to live out their new identity free from the constraints of previous generations.

As firstborns reflect on their roles, they might come to understand that they are not only individuals shaped by familial dynamics but also potential agents of change within those dynamics. They can confront negative patterns and actively choose to model behaviors that reflect God's love and purpose for their families. This recognition emphasizes the pivotal position firstborns hold, often being more visible to their siblings and having the chance to create new traditions and practices within their families. By living out their faith, they can inspire others to break free from patterns of despair and cultivate a legacy of hope.

Faith also equips firstborns to combat spiritual forces that manifest in generational curses. Ephesians 6:12 reminds us that our struggles are not against flesh and blood, but against "the rulers, against the authorities, against the cosmic powers over this present darkness." Firstborns may find themselves uniquely targeted by these spiritual forces due to their roles—often seen as leaders within the family.

Thus, faith acts as both a shield and a sword, empowering these individuals to engage in spiritual warfare on behalf of themselves and their families.

Equipping oneself with knowledge about spiritual authority and the promises of God can dramatically shift the understanding of one's circumstances. Firstborns armed with faith can declare the authority they have in Christ, actively renouncing the curses that might have been passed down. This forceful affirmation of identity in Christ is pivotal in breaking chains that may have persisted for generations. The courage drawn from faith enables them to confront not only the patterns of their families but also any accompanying fears or doubts.

The collective aspect of faith in breaking generational curses cannot be overlooked. While personal faith is essential, communal faith serves as a powerful catalyst for transformation. Firstborns are encouraged to reach out to their faith communities—be it a church, prayer group, or supportive friends—for encouragement in their battles. Sharing their experiences with trusted individuals can lead to collective prayers, mutual support, and accountability, significantly strengthening their resolve to break free from the shackles of familial patterns. In this shared space, firstborns can draw on the strength and testimonies of others, recognizing that they are not alone in facing these challenges.

The culmination of breaking generational curses through faith ultimately leads to a profound sense of hope and renewal. In the life of the believer, old patterns give way to new beginnings, providing a testament to God's sustaining grace. Romans 8:28 offers the encouragement that "in all things God works for the good of those who love him, who have been called according to his purpose." This promise assures firstborns that even the most challenging aspects of their heritage can be redeemed, reshaped, and used for God's glory. Each journey of faith will vary, reflecting individual experiences and contexts. Yet, the essential truth remains—the acknowledgment of the past combined with an unwavering faith in God's promises allows for authentic renewal. Firstborns, in particular, can hold tightly to the conviction that their identities are not determined solely by their birth order or familial struggles, but by their connection to Christ, the Firstborn of all creation. In this relationship, there exists the possibility of breaking generational curses and establishing a new legacy, rich in love, faith, and purpose.

As this subchapter concludes, I extend an invitation to every firstborn grappling with residues of familial pain and burden: Trust in God's power to change your life and the lives of your family. Reflect on the narratives of those who have come before you and recognize the responsibility and significance embedded within your position. With faith as your anchor and guide, you can step boldly into the destiny that has been carved out for you by your Creator, transforming the curses into blessings and shaping a narrative that resonates with hope for generations to come. Let faith in Christ empower you to break free from oppression, reclaim your identity, and shape your family's future through the love and light of God.

CHAPTER 22

THE ROLE OF COMMUNITY

Building Support Systems

For firstborns, the expectation of leadership, responsibility, and success often weighs heavily on their shoulders. In a world where pressures seem to build incessantly from family, society, and even within themselves, the quest for a supportive community becomes crucial. Building strong support systems can act as a lifeline, offering not just encouragement, but also companionship, guidance, and a sense of belonging. This subchapter emphasizes the importance of cultivating environments where firstborns can thrive, grounded in real-life experiences and the transformative power of communal connections.

The significance of family as the foundational community cannot be overstated. For many firstborns, the family represents their first glimpse into relationships, authority, and expectations. This environment is not merely a backdrop but the launching pad for their self-identity. Family dynamics can shape a firstborn's perspective on love, success, and responsibility. Personal stories reveal that for some, the role of the firstborn means shouldering the weight of family expectations, often becoming de facto caretakers or mediators between siblings. The burden can feel overwhelming, yet the family unit retains the unique power to uplift and support its firstborns.

Consider the story of Jessica, a woman who navigated the ups and downs of being the eldest in her family. Growing up, she was often told she needed to be a role model for her younger siblings. It felt pressing and relentless. However, it was within the nurturing embrace of her family community that she found solace. Family gatherings became her refuge, where laughter and shared memories reminded her of her worth beyond performance. It was the shared meals, the inside jokes, and the unconditional love that reconstructed her identity away from rigid expectations.

As firstborns grapple with identity, they may find validation and cheer in their family circles. When they succeed, the family celebrates collectively; when they falter, those same loved ones offer safety nets, encouraging them to rise again. An environment that fosters open dialogue about feelings and stress can be invaluable. Families that operate on trust and support—where encouragement is as fluent as critique—permit firstborns to explore their ambitions without the constant fear of failure.

However, family is not the only pillar of community that can significantly impact a firstborn's journey. The church, often considered a second family, can offer profound support to firstborns navigating their roles both within and outside their families. The church community serves not only as a spiritual guide but also as a network of volunteers, mentors, and friends who share in the journey of faith.

Greg, a firstborn son raised in a church-going family, articulated how pivotal his church community was during his formative years. From youth group meetings to Sunday morning services, he found connection and understanding among peers who were wrestling with similar struggles. The church provided him with mentors who lovingly challenged him while simultaneously nurturing his spirit. Each sermon and fellowship activity offered Greg opportunities to express his hopes and fears openly, as well as the chance to connect with others facing the same pressures.

In a nurturing church community, firstborns often discover a place where they can serve and lead without the added pressure of perfection. They are not merely recipients of support; they are encouraged to contribute their own gifts and strengths. This reciprocal relationship creates a sense of purpose and belonging, vital for reinforcing their identity in Christ as heirs of God's promises.

Additionally, friendship circles—perhaps the most dynamic segment of community—also play a critical role in the development of an individual's life. Friends who understand the challenges and expectations firstborns face can act as anchors amid turbulent waters. These relationships often bring a refreshing perspective, allowing firstborns to engage in genuine conversations free from judgments typically associated with family and authority figures.

Take the story of Amanda, a firstborn who felt the weight of her parents' expectations pulling her down. While her family life was heavy with responsibilities, it was her friendships that offered her the lightness she craved. Amanda's closest friends became a safe space to express fears and aspirations. Their mutual support helped her set boundaries with family and prioritize her mental health. These friendships, forged out of vulnerability and shared experiences, reminded her that she was not alone in her struggles. Through shared moments—late-night talks, group adventures, and heartfelt support—Amanda found strength in her identity, ultimately embracing her flaws and triumphs.

Building these friendships requires intentionality. Firstborns must actively seek out mature relationships that uplift and encourage them. Creating new connections can be daunting, especially for those who feel the need to maintain a façade of having it all together. However, vulnerability is often the key to deeper community ties. It requires acknowledging one's struggles, which can be both scary and liberating. Community thrives on authenticity, and firstborns can cultivate friendships by being open about their fears and challenges. Investing in these relationships can transform the journey of firstborns. Support from peers allows them to balance the expectations thrust upon them with a healthy outlet for expression. Pursuing genuine connections in friendship circles, church communities, and families helps cultivate a rich tapestry of support that can significantly ease the burdens carried by firstborns.

Networking within various spheres broadens the horizons. Seeking connections that align with personal interests—committees, clubs, and volunteer organizations—can be a powerful way for firstborns to nurture their identities beyond family and traditional roles. Engaging with diverse groups also offers firstborns exposure to different worldviews and experiences, encouraging personal growth and resilience.

As firstborns navigate their paths with the support of their communities, they are often better equipped to deal with the pressures of their responsibilities. A robust community provides a safety net, enabling them to embrace their roles without feeling overwhelmed. It reflects the very essence of the body of Christ, where each member contributes their unique gifts to strengthen and uplift one another.

Stronger support systems mean more than emotional backing; they also facilitate spiritual growth. Shared faith experiences—whether in family devotions, church gatherings, or prayer groups—pave the way for deeper connections. Vulnerable sharing of personal testimonies encourages faithfulness and nurtures a sense of belonging. This intersection of faith and community allows firstborns to ground their identities in Christ, dispelling feelings of inadequacy or isolation.

Moreover, involvement in the community offers firstborns the opportunity to transition from feeling like lone warriors battling each challenge to being part of a collaborative effort. Instead of single-handedly bearing the burdens of expectation, firstborns can discover strategic partnerships that empower them to face life's demands head-on.

While building support systems is essential for firstborns, it is equally important to reiterate the ongoing nature of these relationships. Communities thrive when individuals invest time and effort into sustaining connections. This might involve regular gatherings, check-ins, or even informal hangouts, where the joy of companionship can flourish. Enabling these spaces for interaction fosters trust and authenticity, permitting deeper levels of support to emerge.

Sustaining support systems also means cultivating bonds through ups and downs. Firstborns must recognize that real relationships endure challenges. They will inevitably face misunderstandings and conflicts. How these situations are handled can solidify bonds or lead to estrangement. Engaging in healthy communication and finding resolutions when disagreements arise can fortify relationships and establish a foundation of trust.

Furthermore, mentorship should be intentionally sought within these support systems. Firstborns can benefit profoundly from guidance provided by more experienced individuals who have navigated similar challenges. This relational dynamic enriches their journey by offering insights and encouragement. Whether such mentors come from within family circles, faith communities, or peer groups, their wisdom can illuminate paths that firstborns may not readily see.

Looking at different dimensions of community can yield untapped resources for firstborns. Support may come from unexpected places—whether it's an online community, a writer's group, or a sports team. Dedicating energy toward cultivating these relationships can lead to newfound confidence and resilience.

Ultimately, the act of building support systems for firstborns is a sacred responsibility. For individuals who have been given the mantle of leadership and expectation, unlocking the potential for connection can mean the difference between thriving and merely surviving.

Support systems provide a platform through which firstborns can explore their identities, lean into their purpose, and foster a sense of belonging. It allows them to engage in collaborative endeavors that reflect the essence of Christian living.

Therefore, it is crucial not only to seek out these support systems but to actively contribute to them as well. Firstborns must remember that building community is reciprocal; they harness their unique strengths to uplift others while reaping the rewards of connection. As they embrace shared vulnerabilities, celebrate each other's triumphs, and offer encouragement in times of struggle, they create resilient communities that empower everyone involved.

In conclusion, the road traveled by firstborns is often heavy with burdens and expectations, but through the love and support of the communities built around them, they can navigate life's challenges with grace. Whether through the intimate ties of family, the nurturing embrace of church life, or the uplifting presence of friends, the power of supportive communities can reshape firstborn's identities. By investing time and energy into cultivating these relationships and recognizing their seamless importance, firstborns can find strength in unity, overcome personal battles, and embrace the fullness of their design as they embark on their journeys of faith and purpose.

CHAPTER 23

MENTORSHIP AND GUIDANCE

The journey of being a firstborn often comes with a unique set of challenges, expectations, and pressures. As the trailblazers within their families, firstborns frequently find themselves navigating uncharted territory, whether in familial roles, academic pursuits, or social dynamics. In the midst of these challenges, the importance of mentorship cannot be overstated. Mentors, who serve as wise figures offering guidance and support, play a crucial role in helping firstborns manage their responsibilities, develop their identities, and cultivate their spiritual journeys. This subchapter will explore the indispensable role of mentorship in the lives of firstborns, provide testimonials of those who have benefited from such relationships, and encourage readers to actively seek out or become mentors within their communities.

Mentorship is more than a simple advisory relationship; it is a dynamic engagement that fosters growth, resilience, and understanding. A mentor shares not only wisdom and knowledge but also the grace of listening and offering emotional support. For firstborns, who often bear the burdens of leadership and responsibility from a young age, having someone to turn to for direction can make a significant difference.

Biblical mentorship provides a foundational example of how these relationships can transform lives. The Scriptures are rich with accounts of mentorship that show the profound impact one person can have on another. Consider the relationship between Moses and Joshua. Moses guided Joshua through the complexities of leadership, preparing him to lead the Israelites into the Promised Land. Joshua learned from Moses' experiences, mistakes, and triumphs. This two-way relationship not only benefited Joshua but also reinforced Moses' own purpose and calling.

In the New Testament, we see a similar mentorship dynamic in the relationship between Paul and Timothy. Paul, a seasoned apostle, took Timothy under his wing, mentoring him through difficult challenges in the early church. Paul recognized Timothy's potential and became a father figure to him, providing spiritual insight, guidance, and encouragement. Their correspondence, found in the letters of 1 and 2 Timothy, showcases the depth of their relationship and the significant impact mentorship can have on both parties.

These examples illustrate that mentorship is not simply about providing advice; it is about sharing life experiences, nurturing growth, and fostering a sense of identity and purpose. For firstborns, the pressure of expectations can lead to feelings of isolation and stress. A mentor can offer not only guidance but also a listening ear, allowing firstborns to share their struggles and receive wisdom tailored to their unique circumstances.

One powerful testimony comes from Maria, a firstborn who felt overwhelmed by the familial expectations placed upon her. She recounts, "I always felt like I was walking a tightrope—balancing my own desires with the expectations of my family. It wasn't until I found a mentor, someone who had walked a similar path, that I felt understood. This mentor guided Maria through the chaos of her responsibilities and helped her find her identity beyond her role as the firstborn.

Another example is John, who struggled with feelings of inadequacy while trying to uphold the standards he believed were expected of him. "My mentor taught me that it was okay to not have all the answers and to embrace my vulnerabilities," John shares. He highlights a turning point in his life—when his mentor encouraged him to focus not on perfection but on progress. "That perspective shifted everything for me. It allowed me to see my journey as one of growth and learning, rather than a race to meet expectations." These testimonials elucidate the transformative impact of mentorship on firstborns as they navigate their unique struggles. Mentors provide crucial insights and encouragement, helping firstborns reframe their challenges and view them as opportunities for growth. Beyond offering advice, mentors foster resilience in firstborns, reminding them of their inherent worth and potential.

It is not enough, however, to simply wait for mentorship opportunities to arise. Firstborns are encouraged to be proactive in seeking out mentors. This endeavor may involve reaching out to individuals within one's own community, such as teachers, church leaders, or family friends. The act of seeking mentorship requires vulnerability—the willingness to open oneself up to guidance and support.

Additionally, it is important for firstborns to consider the qualities they are looking for in a mentor. Characteristics such as wisdom, empathy, and experience in navigating similar challenges are essential. A mentor should not only provide spiritual insight but also share life experiences that resonate with the mentee's unique journey.

As firstborns seek mentorship, they should also be mindful of their own potential to serve as mentors. The lessons gleaned from their experiences can be invaluable to others. By sharing their insights and struggles, firstborns can create a ripple effect, building a supportive community where individuals are empowered to uplift one another. This concept of communal investment emphasizes that mentorship is a two-way street; both parties benefit from the relationship, resulting in mutual growth and encouragement.

Consider Sarah, a firstborn who, after experiencing her own challenges, felt compelled to mentor younger members of her community. She found that her experiences—whether positive or negative—provided invaluable lessons for those who followed in her footsteps. "I realized that I could use my story to empower others," Sarah states. "When I mentor, I see parts of my younger self in those I guide. It's incredibly fulfilling to help them navigate their own journeys." Sarah's commitment to mentoring not only enriches her life but also creates a sense of purpose, reinforcing her identity as a firstborn.

Moreover, being a mentor fosters personal growth for the mentor as well. Sharing wisdom and guidance with others can lead to deeper self-reflection and growth in one's faith. Mentors are often reminded of their journey, rediscovering the lessons that shaped their paths. This cyclical process of mentorship creates a nurturing environment where wisdom is shared, and experiences are transformed into lessons for others.

Mentorship doesn't have to be formal; it can develop through casual conversations, lunch meetings, or community gatherings. The key is to remain open to the connections that can form. Firstborns should cultivate relationships that foster trust and understanding. Finding a mentor can be as simple as sharing one's journey over coffee or expressing the desire for guidance when engaging with potential mentors.

In addition, structured mentorship programs can provide a more deliberate way for firstborns to connect with experienced mentors. Whether offered through churches, community organizations, or educational institutions, these programs often pair mentors with mentees based on shared interests or challenges. These structured environments help facilitate meaningful relationships that can have a lasting impact on both parties.

Within the context of communities of faith, mentorship can take on an even deeper spiritual dimension. Hebrews 10:24-25 emphasizes the importance of encouraging one another, calling believers to "stir up one another to love and good works." Mentorship aligns with this scriptural call, fostering a spirit of mutual encouragement within the community. When firstborns engage with mentors who emphasize spiritual growth, they enrich their understanding of their faith, aligning their identities with a purpose that extends beyond familial expectations.

In this light, churches can play a vital role in fostering mentorship opportunities. They can facilitate the connection between firstborns and mentors through programs, events, or small group discussions that encourage dialogue about struggles, faith, and purpose. By prioritizing mentorship within the community, church leaders can create an environment where firstborns feel seen, heard, and supported.

As firstborns consider their mentorship journeys, it is important to remember that mentorship is not a one-time event but an ongoing relationship. Building trust and rapport takes time, and both mentors and mentees must commit to the process. Understanding that growth often takes place in increments will allow firstborns to remain patient and engaged in their mentorship experiences.

Ultimately, mentorship serves as an invaluable lifeline, empowering firstborns to navigate the complexities of their lives with resilience and faith. It offers them the opportunity to glean insights from those who have walked similar paths and provides an environment for personal and spiritual growth. Firstborns should seek mentors actively and remain open to the lessons and experiences shared along the way.

As a closing exhortation, firstborns are encouraged to remain vigilant in recognizing their potential as mentors as well. They possess wisdom that can help guide others through their struggles, reinforcing the sense of community investment that is essential for growth and support. By embodying the spirit of mentorship, firstborns can create a legacy of encouragement within their families, churches, and communities, contributing to a cycle of empowerment that uplifts generations to come.

In conclusion, the journey of being a firstborn is often fraught with challenges and expectations. However, with the support of mentors, firstborns can find guidance, encouragement, and community on their paths. The importance of seeking mentorship, providing mentorship, and fostering a community of support cannot be overstated. When firstborns embrace these opportunities, they not only navigate their struggles more effectively but also become agents of transformation for others, reinforcing the collective strength of their communities. The call to mentorship is a call to invest in one another, to build a legacy of support, and to walk together in faith as firstborns journey toward fulfillment and purpose.

CHAPTER 24

CELEBRATING COLLECTIVE STRENGTHS

In the vast tapestry of human experience, communities play a pivotal role in shaping individual lives, particularly for firstborns grappling with unique pressures and expectations. The power of community is magnified when firstborns come together, drawing strength from their shared experiences and collective wisdom. This subchapter seeks to honor and celebrate these collective strengths, emphasizing the importance of experiences, wisdom, and support within firstborn communities. As firstborns unite, they create an environment of encouragement, resilience, and empowerment that allows them not only to thrive individually but also to contribute meaningfully to the growth of the community at large.

To understand the essence of these collective strengths, we must first acknowledge the challenges firstborns often face. From the outset, firstborns frequently assume roles that can lay a heavy burden upon their shoulders. They may find themselves bearing the expectations of their parents and siblings, becoming the trailblazers in the family who set standards and serve as role models. While these responsibilities can foster a sense of pride, they can also lead to immense pressure that can feel isolating. This is where the value of community emerges as a critical counterbalance.

Sharing experiences is perhaps the most profound way firstborn communities forge bonds and build collective strength. The simple act of storytelling allows individuals to lay bare their struggles and victories, creating an open space for empathy and understanding. Each firstborn carries their narrative—stories of triumph and defeat that resonate deeply with others who share similar battles. When firstborns gather, whether physically or virtually, these narratives blend into a rich tapestry of shared experience. They find comfort in knowing that they are not alone in their fears, aspirations, and challenges. For instance, consider a gathering of firstborns at a local church or community center where they share their personal experiences around family dynamics, academic pressures, and the unspoken weight of expectations. In such gatherings, firstborns can relate to an array of experiences: the anxiety of meeting expectations, the demands of being a caretaker, and the joy of paving the way for younger siblings. As they hear one another's stories, they discover common themes that transcend individual circumstances. One may share the pressure of being the first in their family to attend college, while another recounts the haunting fear of failing to live up to parental expectations. These narratives create an unbreakable bond, establishing a foundation whereby individuals uplift each other, recognizing the strength found in vulnerability.

Wisdom often flourishes in environments where experiences are shared. Within firstborn communities, older firstborns can offer insights and guidance to those still navigating their roles. This transfer of wisdom is invaluable, as it builds on lessons learned through lived experiences while providing a roadmap for facing challenges ahead. Younger firstborns can benefit immensely from the counsel of those who have journeyed down similar paths, highlighting the interconnectedness of their experiences. Mentorship emerges as a powerful mechanism within these communities, amplifying the strengths of the collective and ensuring that wisdom flows freely.

For example, consider a firstborn mentoring program within a church community where seasoned firstborns take on the role of guides for younger members. Through structured mentorship, they can share their triumphs and pitfalls, offering insights that can inspire and equip the next generation. This creates an enriching environment where growth is not linear but cyclical, bending back on itself to strengthen the entire community. The passing of knowledge and experience fosters deep connections and reinforces the notion that firstborns, despite their differences, can emerge stronger together.

In addition to sharing experiences and wisdom, the support that exists within firstborn communities acts as a powerful catalyst for communal growth. The challenges faced are often heavy, and the burden of carrying them alone can be overwhelming. By fostering a culture of support and understanding, firstborns are better equipped to address their struggles. This support often manifests in various forms—emotional, spiritual, or practical. For instance, firstborns may gather to pray for one another during times of distress, forming solidarity that envelops them in the love and encouragement of shared faith.

Practical support can also take the form of collective problem- solving. Within groups, firstborns can brainstorm solutions to navigate shared challenges such as stress from school or work, family dynamics, or spiritual dilemmas. They may organize study groups, workshops, or fundraising events, drawing on each member's unique strengths and abilities. Collaboratively, they can mitigate their challenges, highlighting the notion that no firstborn should ever tackle life's battles alone.

Reflecting on one's contributions brings us to the heart of community ownership among firstborns. Each member contributes a vital piece to the collective puzzle, ensuring the community thrives. Acknowledging one's role helps foster a sense of responsibility and commitment to the group, reinforcing that everyone plays an integral part. Firstborns should take time to reflect on the gifts they bring to their communities—be it leadership, compassion, creativity, or determination.

Take, for instance, the firstborn in a musical family who organizes a charity concert to raise funds for a local cause. Not only does their leadership create an opportunity for others to contribute their talents, but it also channels collective energy into something meaningful, fostering community pride and reinforcing the bonds among members. This act of ownership highlights the potential that firstborns possess to drive positive change within their communities. The strength of collaboration can be seen through various successful initiatives among firstborns. One such example is a community project where firstborns come together to support families in need during the holiday season.

They might run a food drive, collecting donations to assemble care packages for those less fortunate. The combination of their efforts demonstrates the power of collective action, where the impact is amplified through their unity. Such projects do more than serve those in need; they reinforce relationships among firstborns, creating a shared purpose that fosters lasting connections.

To further explore the notion of collective strengths, it is essential to consider the role of celebration within firstborn communities. Acknowledging each other's achievements cultivates an atmosphere of encouragement and affirmation. When firstborns celebrate their milestones—be it graduations, promotions, or personal accomplishments—they not only honor their journeys but also inspire those around them. Recognizing successes strengthens the resolve to continue pressing forward, even when faced with adversity.

Consider the poignant moment of a firstborn's graduation. The celebration, marked by family gatherings and community events, becomes an occasion for the entire network to acknowledge the hard work and determination invested in that achievement. The graduate stands not just as an individual but as a representative of their community, illustrating that their accomplishments contribute to the collective narrative. Through such acknowledgments, firstborns collectively reinforce the importance of perseverance, resilience, and shared joy.

Beyond individual milestones, community celebrations that highlight collective achievements reinforce a sense of belonging and pride. Annual gatherings, retreats, or community fairs provide a platform to celebrate the strengths of the firstborn community. These events are vital not only for reflection and joy but also for reconnection and rejuvenation. Amidst the chaos of daily life, there is immense value in taking a step back to celebrate the collective journey.

As firstborns come together, they can create traditions, rituals, and celebrations that honor their unique identities and experiences. These gatherings foster connections that go beyond surface interactions, inviting deeper relationships rooted in mutual support and understanding. By cultivating a sense of pride in their identity, firstborns can draw strength from one another, positioning themselves to overcome challenges faced individually and collectively.

Acknowledging successes also offers a powerful opportunity to inspire newcomers to the community. When younger firstborns witness the triumphs of their older counterparts, they are motivated to pursue their aspirations with vigor. This chain of inspiration fuels a culture of ambition and hope, emphasizing an essential lesson: the journey is made richer when traveled together.

While the collective strengths of firstborns are profound, it is equally important to recognize the potential pitfalls that may arise within communities. Competition and jealousy can sometimes seep into interactions, especially when individuals feel threatened or overshadowed by their peers. However, firstborns can combat these negative dynamics by committing to a culture of support and encouragement. This requires conscious effort—by fostering an atmosphere where everyone's achievements are celebrated, firstborns can collectively rise above these pitfalls and contribute positively to one another's growth.

In cultivating an empowered community, firstborns must actively work to engage others, encouraging participation and investment from every member. Whether through social gatherings, service opportunities, or collaborative projects, the goal is to create an inclusive space where everyone feels valued and heard. As they collectively work toward this goal, firstborns can embrace their unique challenges and triumphs, inherently strengthening their bonds.

As we celebrate the collective strengths within firstborn communities, it is crucial to reframe the narrative surrounding their roles. Rather than viewing firstborns solely as leaders or burden-bearers, they can be seen as integral to the collective identity, fostering relationships imbued with strength, wisdom, and vulnerability. By sharing stories, offering support, and celebrating triumphs, firstborns help cultivate a community that thrives on connection and acceptance.

Ultimately, the journey of the firstborn is not meant to be a solitary one; it is enriched through the shared experiences and contributions of each member in the community. The spirit of togetherness amplifies their individual and collective strengths, reinforcing the idea that firstborns can weather any storm as long as they stand united. As they continue to celebrate their journeys and offer support to one another, they pave the way for future generations of firstborns to thrive in an environment of unwavering strength and encouragement.

In conclusion, the collective strengths found within firstborn communities are profound and transformative. By sharing experiences, wisdom, and support, firstborns create an environment that contributes to individual and communal growth. The responsibility lies within each member to reflect on their contributions, actively engage in their community, and celebrate each other's victories. Together, they can navigate the complexities of their roles and emerge as a powerful force for good, illuminating the path forward for others while honoring their unique journeys. As firstborns learn to embrace their identities in this communal context, they realize that they are not just agents of their destinies but integral threads woven into the larger tapestry of faith, hope, and resilience.

CHAPTER 25

LIVING IN VICTORY

Embracing a Mindset of Victory

In the journey of life, the way we think can shape our reality more than we realize. This notion is particularly poignant for firstborns, who often carry the heavy mantle of expectations, responsibilities, and roles within the family and society. The phenomenon of feeling overwhelmed, pressured, or even defeated can easily seep into the minds of those who hold such titles. However, the message of Christ offers a radical transformation of this mindset—a call to embrace a victorious identity grounded in faith.

Adopting a victorious mindset through faith in Christ is not merely an elusive abstract; it is a concrete reality available to all who believe. Firstborns need to recognize that their worth and identity are anchored not in familial roles or societal pressures but in the unconditional love of God, who sees them as His beloved creation. Scripture poignantly affirms this truth: "But thanks be to God, who gives us the victory through our Lord Jesus Christ" (1 Corinthians 15:57).

Understanding that victory is a given, through Christ, can shift perspectives from feelings of inadequacy to a posture of empowerment. This transition is not automatic; it requires intentionality, prayer, and an inner willingness to accept God's promises. Through various biblical principles, we can see how a transformational shift occurs when we align our thoughts with God's truth.

In Romans 12:2, we are urged: "Do not be conformed to this world, but be transformed by the renewal of your mind." This renewal process is crucial for firstborns who may feel elevated yet burdened by their position. It starts with recognizing the deceptions that often cloud our vision—the lies that say we are less than, that we will fail, or that our worth is contingent on our achievements or the expectations of others. By confronting these lies with biblical truths, firstborns can begin to embrace a mindset that is victorious rather than defeated.

One striking example of a character who embodied this victorious mindset is David, a shepherd boy chosen to be king. Remember the story of David and Goliath? As a young shepherd, David faced ridicule and doubt, especially from his own brothers, who were experienced warriors. They saw the giant Goliath as an unbeatable foe, and so did the entire Israelite army. Yet, David, with his heart aligned with God's and armed with a mindset that grasped the victory in God's promises, rose to face Goliath. He declared, "The battle is the Lord's" (I Samuel 17:47). This realization empowered him to act in faith, and ultimately, he secured a victory that changed the fate of a nation.

David's story beckons firstborns to realize that even when the odds seem insurmountable, their identity in Christ empowers them to face their challenges. Whether it's challenging familial dynamics, expectations at school, or societal pressures, the truth remains unchanged: they are conquerors through Christ who strengthens them (Philippians 4:13). This victory is not conditional upon their performance but rooted in a loving relationship with their creator. A powerful testimony that illustrates this transformation comes from Jessica, a firstborn who thought her worth was based solely on her achievements. As a child, she felt the pressure to excel in academic and leadership roles, believing that failure to meet these expectations would lead to disappointment, not only for herself but for her family. It wasn't until she faced significant struggles at university that she began to question her identity.

One difficult semester brought her to the point of emotional collapse. It was during nights filled with tears and frustration that she began to seek God deeply for clarity. In her quest, she stumbled upon Romans 8:37, which states, "No, in all these things we are more than conquerors through him who loved us." As she meditated on this verse, the message began to resonate deeply in her spirit. She saw for the first time that her identity as a firstborn was not as an unyielding achiever but as a beloved daughter of the King, destined for greatness not through personal merit but through God's grace.

This realization did not eliminate her desire to succeed, but it changed the motivation behind it. No longer was she chasing perfection; rather, she began to pursue excellence as an outflow of her relationship with God. She learned to embrace setbacks as opportunities for growth rather than as definitions of her worth. This pivotal shift enabled her to approach challenges with faith and to encourage others around her, highlighting the infectious power of a victorious mindset.

For firstborns grappling with the burdens of expectation, embracing a mindset of victory may require a deliberate reprogramming of their thoughts. The enemy wants them to feel defeated, overwhelmed, and distant from God's love. However, the Spirit of God calls them to rise above these lies.

Philippians 4:8 offers practical guidance for cultivating this mindset: "Finally, brothers, whatever is true, whatever is honorable, whatever is just, whatever is pure, whatever is lovely, whatever is commendable, if there is any excellence, if there is anything worthy of praise, think about these things." By meditating on what is true and good, firstborns can reclaim their mental and emotional landscapes. It is equally vital for firstborns to find community support as they navigate this path of renewal. Sharing experiences with others who understand the unique pressures faced can provide comfort and encouragement. In a small group or church fellowship, firstborns can voice their struggles and feel validated, realizing they are not alone in their challenges. Collectively, they can remind one another of the truth of Scripture, reinforcing each other's identities as victorious children of God.

Firstborns are also called into positions of influence, often naturally becoming leaders. This leadership can lead to feelings of isolation or self-doubt. In these moments, they must remember the source of their strength. "In all your ways acknowledge Him, and He will make straight your paths" (Proverbs 3:6). Acknowledging God in every endeavor empowers them to embrace their leadership not as a burden but as an opportunity to reflect His glory.

Another dimension in embracing a victorious mindset is the practice of gratitude. In 1 Thessalonians 5:18, we are instructed to "give thanks in all circumstances." Cultivating a grateful heart can help firstborns shift focus away from what they lack or the pressures they face, placing their attention instead on God's faithfulness and blessings. Gratitude opens a pathway to positivity, allowing for an appreciation of even the smallest victories in their lives.

The fulfillment of God's promises will not always transpire in the way firstborns envision. However, having a mindset centered on victory will enable them to trust that God is working even through their trials. James 1:2-3 encourages believers to "count it all joy when you meet trials of various kinds." This invitation to joy does not negate the pain or difficulty but rather affirms that God is present during these times.

A deeply transformative exercise involves journaling this journey. Firstborns can reflect on their struggles, faith declarations, and moments of victory. By documenting their stories, they can build a clearer understanding of God's hand in their lives. Reflecting upon past experiences will continually remind them of God's faithfulness and grace, solidifying their identity as victors.

As this subchapter draws to a close, let it be noted that embracing a mindset of victory is an ongoing journey. It is not a destination, but a daily choice empowered by faith. Firstborns must actively choose to fix their eyes on Jesus, who is the pioneer and perfecter of their faith (Hebrews 12:2). Daily declarations of Scripture can reinforce this mindset, equipping them to confront challenges boldly.

To assist in internalizing this victorious mindset, consider the following reflective prompts:

- What lies have you believed about your identity or worth? Write them down and counter each with a corresponding biblical truth.- Reflect on a challenging situation you faced recently. How did your mindset influence your response? What could you do differently in the future?

- Identify one area where you can practice gratitude today. Write a list of things you are thankful for and allow this practice to reshape your perspective.- Who in your life can you share your struggles with? How can you establish a support system that uplifts you in your journey?

- Write a prayer declaring your identity as a conqueror through Christ. Affirm your trust in God's plans for your life, regardless of the circumstances.

In these reflective moments, firstborns can begin to shift their perspectives from defeat to empowerment, uncovering the divine potential within them. Empowered by Christ's victory, may they walk confidently into their future, recognizing that they are not just firstborns but deeply loved children of God destined for greatness in His kingdom. Embracing this mindset will catalyze a whirlwind of transformation, not only in their lives but also in the lives of those they impact. By choosing to live in victory, they align with their true identity and purpose, embracing the abundant life God has promised.

CHAPTER 26

PRACTICAL STRATEGIES FOR DAILY VICTORY

L iving victoriously is not merely a lofty aspiration; it requires deliberate action, intentionality, and a commitment to cultivating the right mindset and habits. For firstborns, who often shoulder significant expectations and responsibilities, adopting practical strategies for daily victory becomes essential. In this subchapter, we will explore actionable steps that empower firstborns to embrace their identity in Christ, navigate life's challenges with resilience, and maintain a perspective of hope and optimism.

First and foremost, the power of prayer cannot be overstated. Prayer serves as a lifeline to God, allowing firstborns to express their thoughts, fears, and desires while inviting divine guidance and strength into their daily lives. It is essential to establish a consistent prayer routine, one that reflects a genuine, relational dialogue with God. Here are some practical recommendations to enhance the effectiveness of prayer in the journey toward victory:

Set Aside Dedicated Time: Carving out specific moments throughout the day for prayer helps prioritize a relationship with God. Consider morning devotionals to set a positive tone for the day or evening reflections to help process the day's experiences.

Create a Prayer Journal: Documenting prayers and reflections in a dedicated journal enhances the practice by providing a tangible way to track spiritual growth and witness answers to prayers over time. Marking significant milestones and breakthroughs can bolster faith when challenges arise.

Engage in Intercessory Prayer: Praying for others fosters a spirit of generosity and compassion while shifting the focus away from one's problems. Firstborns can create a prayer team within their community, sharing prayer requests and uplifting one another in their journeys.

Practice Spontaneous Prayer: Beyond formal prayer sessions, spontaneous prayers throughout the day can help maintain a connection with God. Whispering quick prayers during challenging moments or expressing gratitude for blessings in real-time reinforces a mindset of awareness and reliance on Christ.

Utilize Scripture in Prayer: Incorporating scripture into prayers reinforces the truth of God's word while aligning intentions with divine promises. Firstborns can draw on specific verses related to their situations, reminding themselves of God's faithfulness.

In addition to prayer, positive affirmations are a vital strategy for combating negative self-talk and reinforcing a mindset of victory. Firstborns often grapple with feelings of inadequacy, driven by the weight of their responsibilities and expectations. Positive affirmations offer a remedy by nurturing self-worth and fostering empowerment. Here's how to effectively integrate positive affirmations into daily life:

Identify Truths about Identity: Begin by reflecting on biblical truths that affirm identity in Christ. Verses such as Ephesians 1:4-5 and 2 Corinthians 5:17 remind believers of their worth, purpose, and transformation through faith. Writing these truths down can create powerful affirmations.

Create a Daily Affirmation Routine: Firstborns can start each day by reciting affirmations aloud, declaring their value in God's eyes. Emphasizing phrases like "I am loved," "I am capable," and "I am an overcomer" serves as a powerful foundation for the day ahead. Utilize Visual Reminders: Placing written affirmations in visible locations, such as mirrors, workspaces, or on the refrigerator, serves as a constant reminder of one's identity. These visual cues can uplift spirits during difficult moments and reinforce positive thought patterns.

Engage in Community Affirmation: Encouraging accountability through community settings can amplify the impact of affirmations. Firstborns can engage friends or family members to share affirmations and collectively speak words of encouragement, reinforcing a sense of belonging and support.

Monitor Self-Talk: An essential aspect of incorporating affirmations is being mindful of internal dialogue. Firstborns can challenge negative thoughts by replacing them with affirmations, recognizing that the mind has the power to shape actions and emotions.

Surrounding oneself with uplifting influences is another pivotal strategy for living victoriously. The company firstborns keep significantly impacts their outlook and emotional well-being. Negative or toxic relationships can drain energy, foster feelings of inadequacy, and hamper spiritual growth. Here are practices to cultivate positive influences in daily life:

Evaluate Relationships: Firstborns should assess their current relationships, discerning which connections uplift and encourage versus those that drain their energy. It may be necessary to distance oneself from negative influences or engage in open conversations to address concerns.

Seek Out Supportive Communities: Frequently, finding a church or community group that aligns with personal values and beliefs can provide a nurturing environment for growth. Firstborns are encouraged to participate in Bible studies, fellowship groups, or mentorship programs that foster spiritual and emotional development.

Invest in Mentoring Relationships: Establishing connections with mentors—individuals who have experience and wisdom—can offer invaluable guidance. Firstborns can seek mentors within their churches or communities who can provide support and encouragement in their journeys toward victory.

Create a Positive Input Diet: Surrounding oneself with uplifting media—books, podcasts, music, and positive socialmedia accounts—can dramatically influence mood and motivation. Firstborns should curate their input, focusing on content that inspires and nurtures their faith.

Practice Gratitude: Engaging in a daily gratitude practice allows firstborns to maintain a focus on positivity. Recognizing moments of joy and blessings, no matter how small, can help shift perspective. This practice connects with the biblical idea of thankfulness, reinforcing faith and appreciation for God's goodness.

Incorporating these strategies into daily life requires intentionality and commitment, but the benefits can be transformative. By adopting a consistent prayer life, practicing positive affirmations, and surrounding themselves with uplifting influences, firstborns can cultivate a mindset that thrives on victory.

To illustrate the impact of these strategies, let us consider a few personal testimonies that highlight their effectiveness.

Sarah, a firstborn from a family of three, often felt overwhelmed by her responsibilities as the eldest. Juggling her job, family obligations, and personal goals led to constant high stress and anxiety. It wasn't until she began a disciplined prayer routine that she noticed significant changes. By committing to morning prayers and journaling her thoughts, Sarah found clarity and peace in uncertain situations. "Prayer became my refuge, a space where I could unload my worries and invite God into my chaos," she shared.

In addition to prayer, Sarah decided to incorporate positive affirmations into her daily routine. She began each morning by reciting affirmations before her bathroom mirror. "I am loved. I have purpose. I can conquer this day." These affirmations gradually changed her inner dialogue, helping her embrace her unique role without excessive pressure. "Looking at myself and saying those words empowered me," she reflected. "It wasn't just about being perfect; it was about being authentic and finding strength in God's design for me."

Another testimony comes from Michael, a firstborn who struggled with feelings of inadequacy due to constant comparisons to his siblings. Recognizing the need for uplifting influences in his life, Michael sought out mentorship from a respected leader in his church. Their conversations revolved around building confidence in his abilities and understanding his worth in God's eyes. "Having a mentor changed everything for me," Michael explained. "It helped me see the potential that others saw in me, even when I couldn't." Michael consciously started curating his media consumption, filling his time with podcasts and audiobooks focused on personal and spiritual development. He fostered connections with friends who encouraged him in his faith, ultimately enabling him to step confidently into his calling. "Community has been a game changer," he shared. "Surrounding myself with positive people who believed in me allowed me to take risks and embrace the firstborn's mantle rather than dread it."

While the journey of living victoriously may come with challenges, these practical strategies empower firstborns to cultivate habits that reinforce faith. The transformation starts with acknowledging one's identity in Christ, affirming it daily, engaging in meaningful prayer, and surrounding oneself with positive influences.

Moreover, daily victory requires ongoing attention, assessment, and adjustment. It involves being mindful of the language used, the company kept, and the practices adopted. Creating new habits takes time, so allow for grace in the process while remaining vigilant against negative thoughts and influences. Every step taken toward adopting these strategies is a victory in itself.

Finally, creating a culture of encouragement among firstborns can amplify the impact of these strategies. Sharing experiences, testimonies, and victories within acommunity fosters an environment where individuals inspire one another to act in faith. They can create groups focused on accountability, encouragement, and shared challenges, thus becoming a source of strength and support.

In conclusion, living victoriously is a continuous journey encompassing prayer, affirmations, and surrounding oneself with uplifting influences. Practical strategies serve as tools to navigate daily challenges while nurturing a victorious mindset. Every firstborn carries a unique calling and potential that aligns with God's purpose. By committing to these practices, firstborns can claim their victory, live boldly in their identity, and inspire others to do the same, contributing to a legacy of faith and resilience for generations to come.

CHAPTER 27

THE IMPACT OF VICTORY ON OTHERS

Living in victory is a profound journey marked by personal transformation, and its impact extends far beyond the individual who experiences it. For firstborns, often tasked with the weight of expectations and responsibilities, the triumphs gathered throughout their lives serve as powerful testimonies that can influence those around them. When firstborns embrace their identities in Christ and navigate their lives through a lens of victory, they become catalysts for change, embodying a ripple effect of positivity and faith that can uplift families, friends, and communities.

The narrative of victory is woven intricately into the fabric of relationships. Firstborns, whether through their leadership in familial settings, their roles in peer groups, or their positions in the workplace, have the potential to inspire others simply by living out their experiences of faith. Overcoming challenges and embracing a victorious mindset can lead to profound transformations not only within their lives but also within the lives of others who witness their journeys.

Consider the story of David, a firstborn whose life has been marked by struggles with self-doubt and fear of failure. Growing up in a household where expectations were high, David often felt the pressure to achieve and excel in every area. However, through a series of hardships, including academic setbacks and personal losses, David found solace in his faith. He discovered that true victory lies in leaning on Christ rather than striving alone. As he shifted his perspective, embracing God's promises, something remarkable happened: David began to share his story.

His vulnerability resonated within his community. Friends who once felt isolated in their struggles found a kindred spirit in David.

As he openly spoke about his faith journey, sharing his victories and setbacks alike, he encouraged others to embrace their vulnerabilities. This led to a support network where people found strength in each other's stories. The ripple effect of David's victory inspired his peers to engage in their own journeys of faith—transforming their understanding of resilience and community.

This scenario exemplifies how one person's journey can create a wave of encouragement. Firstborns often hold a unique position within families that predisposes them to be leaders, whether by birthright or through the expectations placed upon them. Their victories can serve as landmark moments for younger siblings and peers, providing concrete examples of how faith can lead to triumph in life's challenges. The emotional and spiritual upliftment that firstborns can provide is potent, serving as a reminder of the potential we all have to inspire those around us.

In cultures around the world, firstborns are often seen as trailblazers. In many African cultures, for instance, the firstborn son typically carries a significant load of family expectations, often serving as a model for younger siblings. When such a firstborn succeeds by overcoming difficulties through the power of faith, their journey becomes a story of hope for the family. Their ability to rise above adversity not only instills confidence in their younger siblings but also promotes a sense of shared legacy. This shared legacy becomes the foundation on which the next generation builds their narrative, demonstrating the interconnectedness of personal victory and collective hope.

Throughout history, we have seen countless instances of firstborns embodying the role of light-bearers. In the Christian context, we can look to biblical figures such as Joseph—the favored son. Despite facing betrayal, imprisonment, and abandonment, Joseph's faith remained steadfast. His story culminates in an incredible victory not only for himself but for his entire family during a time of famine. The way Joseph navigated his challenges—with integrity, faith, and grace—served as an inspiration to his family and eventually led to the reconciliation of deep familial rifts. This biblical narrative illustrates that when a firstborn lives in victory, the resulting impact can resonate for generations.

A prominent example in contemporary society is that of Brenda, a firstborn who used her experience of overcoming domestic struggles to establish a community program aimed at youth mentorship. Brenda faced immense difficulty in her home life. However, through her faith and determination, she sought to create a brighter future for herself and her siblings. Recognizing the strength of community support, she drew upon her journey to mentor young women facing similar challenges. Her influence inspired these young women to discover their self-worth and strive for their goals.

Brenda's victories became a beacon of light. Her ability to transform pain into purpose encouraged her mentees to reach for their dreams, creating an ongoing cycle of empowerment. They, too, began to reach out to others in their communities, forging connection and support. The ripple effect of Brenda's journey continues to inspire not just one or two individuals but entire communities to believe in the possibilities that arise when faith and victory intermingle.

The effectiveness of a firstborn's testimony in influencing others can be attributed to their authenticity. People naturally gravitate toward narratives of triumph because they evoke hope—an undeniable promise of change. The heartfelt stories of personal struggle, combined with the unwavering faith that led to victory, resonate deeply. This authenticity is vital for creating connections across varied age groups and backgrounds.

As firstborns navigate their journeys and share their stories of victory, they not only shine a light on the path of personal growth but also provide an understanding that encourages others to embark on their journeys. Reflection, vulnerability, and authenticity all serve to build trust, open lines of communication, and foster a culture of encouragement.

In many ways, victory, when shared, becomes a communal treasure. The stories of triumph encourage conversations around faith, resilience, and healing. They create spaces for individuals to process their challenges openly, cultivate understanding, and find solidarity in shared experiences. When firstborns embrace their roles as beacons of hope, they ignite a movement of positivity that resounds through families, friendships, and communities.

However, with this unique role comes the responsibility of intention. Firstborns must actively choose to share their victories and uplift others. The call to action is not passive; it must be executed with a sense of urgency and commitment. It invites self-reflection about how one's victories are positioned within the broader community. Are firstborns actively sharing their journeys? Are they proactive in reaching out to inspire others? This introspection paves the way for a deeper understanding of how powerfully one's actions can impact collective well-being.

Being a beacon of hope involves intentionally uplifting others. Firstborns are encouraged to seek opportunities to engage with those who can benefit from encouragement, mentorship, or simply a listening ear. Engaging in community service, mentorship programs, or church activities allows firstborns to integrate their journey into a larger narrative of hope and transformation.

Furthermore, this involvement can foster connections that create safe environments for open dialogue about personal struggles, encouraging collective healing and encouragement within communities. Establishing these relationships is crucial; by forming communities built around shared victories and challenges, firstborns can manifest a culture where collective strength thrives.

As the ripple effect broadens, the impact of living in victory transcends individual lives, creating a culture that acknowledges struggle while celebrating triumph. The hope instilled by shared victories can lead to collaborative efforts aimed at uplifting entire communities, forging a better understanding of faith, resilience, and shared humanity.

Firstborns are encouraged to document their journeys through various platforms—be it blogs, social media, or community gatherings—to multiply their impact. By sharing personal testimonies, firstborns can inspire others to engage in their narratives, fostering a collective atmosphere where stories are shared, struggles are understood, and victories are celebrated.

Moreover, the emphasis on cultivating community becomes paramount. When firstborns come together to share their experiences, they invite opportunities for collaboration, bonding, and growth. These gatherings serve as transformative spaces where victories can be acknowledged and collective narratives can emerge, strengthening the web of support that firstborns create together.

Ultimately, the challenge for readers extends beyond individual narratives; it encompasses the forthcoming potential to uplift others within their spheres of influence. The invitation is to actively participate in the journey of liberation from burdens and embrace a newfound identity rooted in victory. When firstborns consciously share their stories and extend hands of support, the impact can reverberate throughout communities—transforming individual struggles into collective victories.

As the journey of living in victory leads to a deeper understanding of the purpose and potential of firstborns, the overarching message is clear: victory isn't merely an individual accomplishment; it is a shared journey marked by hope, faith, and connection. By embracing this narrative, firstborns can navigate their lives and the lives of those around them in a way that transforms the ordinary into extraordinary, together illuminating paths of hope for generations to come.

CHAPTER 28

A CALL TO ACTION

Embracing Your Identity

Embracing your identity as a firstborn carries profound significance. The weight of expectation, the responsibility of leadership within the family, and the call to fulfill a unique purpose can all feel overwhelming. Yet, it is crucial to understand that your identity is not merely a set of burdensome obligations, but a beautiful calling bestowed upon you by God. This subchapter serves as a compelling invitation to embrace that identity with confidence and grace.

As firstborns, there is a distinct role you play—not just within your family but in the larger tapestry of life. From the very beginning of biblical history, firstborns have been set apart. They were the inheritors of blessings, the bearers of promises, and the leaders among their siblings. This rich heritage continues to resonate today, reminding you of the incredible potential that lies within you.

Consider the biblical account of Joseph, the son of Jacob. Despite being the favored child, he faced tremendous challenges, including betrayal by his brothers, slavery, and imprisonment. Yet, through all of these trials, he remained steadfast in his identity as a child of God. His experiences shaped him, but they did not define him; his identity as a firstborn son and a man of faith did. When Joseph eventually rose to power in Egypt, he used his position to save his family and countless others from famine. His journey illustrates that embracing your identity can lead not only to personal victory but also to the restoration of those around you.

To embrace your identity as a firstborn, it is essential to recognize the unique qualities you possess. Firstborns often exhibit traits such as responsibility, diligence, and leadership. These characteristics are not merely coincidental; they are part of the divine design crafted by God. The apostle Paul reminds us in Ephesians 2:10 that "we are God's handiwork, created in Christ Jesus to do good works, which God prepared in advance for us to do." You are a masterpiece, created for a purpose.

However, societal expectations and familial pressures can cloud your understanding of this identity. Firstborns frequently feel the need to be perfect: to excel academically, to lead with unwavering confidence, and to always be the example for others. It is essential to understand that perfection is not a prerequisite for fulfilling your divine calling. Acknowledging your weaknesses can lead to deeper connections with God and ultimately lead you to embrace the grace that sufficiency brings. The journey of faith is not merely about achieving perfection; it is also about learning, growing, and relying on God's strength in times of weakness.

Consider the story of Moses, who was also a firstborn. He grew up in the Egyptian palace but faced a series of failures that led him to flee into the wilderness. It was there, after years of feeling inadequate, that God called him to liberate the Israelites. Moses initially resisted his calling, expressing doubt about his abilities. However, God reassured him that His presence would go with him. Just like Moses, you may face moments of doubt, wondering if you can fulfill the role God has for you. Yet, the truth is, God does not call the equipped; He equips the called.

Reflect on your own experiences as a firstborn. What qualities do you see in yourself? What dreams have you tucked away out of fear of inadequacy? By contemplating these questions, you can begin to uncover the layers of your true identity. Are you a nurturer like Miriam, who protected her brother Moses? Are you a peacemaker, striving to hold the family together, even when tensions rise? Or perhaps you have the vision and courage of a leader, born to guide others into their destinies.

In addition to recognizing your inherent qualities, it is essential to embrace the authority that comes with your identity. As a firstborn, you are not only an individual with responsibilities; you are also an anchor for your siblings and a catalyst for change. This authority is not about control; it is about influence—impacting those around you through love, wisdom, and the grace of God. Romans 8:37 reminds us, "No, in all these things we are more than conquerors through him who loved us." You have the potential to impact your family and community positively; your actions can create a ripple effect of healing and hope.

One practical way to step into your identity is to actively engage in service. Whether through mentorship, community outreach, or simply being available for your siblings, your contributions can reflect your understanding of your role. As firstborns lead by example, you embody the love and compassion of Christ, illustrating what it means to live out this identity effectively.

As you embrace your identity, it is important to remember that you are not alone in this journey. God has placed people in your life—friends, family, mentors, and even fellow firstborns—who can support and encourage you. Engage with your community, share your struggles, and build relationships founded on trust and understanding. This network of support will be instrumental as you navigate the highs and lows of your journey, encouraging you to embrace your identity even when the path is challenging.

Reflecting on your journey is an essential step in fully embracing your identity. Take time to journal your thoughts and feelings about being a firstborn. What has been the greatest challenge you've faced in this role? What moments have brought you the most joy? By putting pen to paper, you can articulate the emotions tied to your identity, helping you process your experiences and recognize God's hand at work in your life.

Consider the impact of your story on those around you. When you authentically embrace your identity as a firstborn, you encourage others to do the same. Your willingness to share your journey—both the successes and the struggles—can provide comfort and hope for others grappling with similar challenges. God often uses our stories to uplift and inspire, turning our scars into testimonies that glorify Him.

In embracing your identity, it is crucial to approach your calling with a spirit of humility. Jesus, the ultimate example of leadership, embodied humility throughout His life. Philippians 2:6-7 states that Jesus "being in very nature God, did not consider equality with God something to be used to his own advantage; rather, he made himself nothing by taking the very nature of a servant." As you step into your role as a firstborn, remember to approach your responsibilities with the same humility and servant-hearted attitude. This will cultivate a spirit of grace and integrity within you, further solidifying your identity in Christ.

Moreover, it is essential to embrace the power of prayer in this journey. Through prayer, you can seek God's guidance and strength, enabling you to walk in your true identity with confidence. Prayer shapes our perspectives and reminds us of the promises God has for each of us. Moreover, it creates a space for divine communication, allowing God's voice to guide you.

As you navigate your calling, it is also worth noting that embracing your identity is a continuous journey—one that unfolds over time as you grow in your faith. It may look different at various stages of your life, and that's perfectly normal. Your identity as a firstborn is intertwined with your identity in Christ, which grows and evolves as you deepen your relationship with Him.

The willingness to embrace your identity is a significant step towards living out the calling that God has placed on your life. When you accept who you are—a beloved child of God, uniquely created with intentions and purpose—you free yourself from the burden of expectations or comparisons. This acceptance nurtures your growth and empowers you to flourish in your role.

Reflective questions to ponder as you embrace your identity might include:

What does being a firstborn mean to me personally?

How do my qualities enhance my role within my family and community?

In what ways can I actively serve and support others as a firstborn? What fears or doubts do I need to surrender to God in order to embrace my identity fully?

How can I establish and strengthen my support network as I walk in my identity?

What steps can I take to celebrate my unique contributions and the impact I have on those around me?

What biblical promises can I hold onto that reinforce my worth and identity in Christ?

Taking time to reflect on these questions will guide you on your journey of embracing your identity as a firstborn. Recognize that this journey is not solely about the destination; it is also about the process of growing, maturing, and discovering the person God has designed you to be.

In conclusion, embracing your identity as a firstborn is not a passive endeavor; it is an active stance of acceptance, courage, and purpose. In doing so, you walk confidently in the unique role God has given you, unleashing your potential to impact your family, community, and the world. As you recognize your worth, you also illuminate the path for others, encouraging them to embrace their identities and fulfill their divine purposes. The journey of a firstborn is, after all, a journey of hope, triumph, and profound significance—a legacy shaped by the hands of the Master Creator.

CHAPTER 29

MAKING A POSITIVE IMPACT

As firstborns, many have been made acutely aware of the weight of expectations placed upon them, whether from family, society, or even themselves. But within that weight lies an incredible gift—a calling to make a positive impact on the world. Recognizing and embracing this potential allows firstborns to step into roles that foster change, encourage others, and impart lasting legacies. The journey toward fulfilling this purpose is not just about ambition but about aligning with God's will to serve others and build meaningful communities. At the heart of this calling lies the understanding that firstborns are often endowed with unique abilities, talents, and insights. These gifts, whether they manifest as leadership skills, creativity, compassion, or the ability to inspire, come with a divine mandate to act.

The concept of being a firstborn transcends biological birth order; it encapsulates a broader narrative of prominence, influence, and responsibility. Firstborns—both in families and in broader societal contexts—are often viewed as leaders and trailblazers. This is a role they can seize to lead others toward hope, healing, and upliftment. Consider the biblical examples of impactful firstborns who harnessed their gifts for the greater good. Joseph, the son of Jacob, is one of the most notable figures. Despite facing numerous challenges, including betrayal by his brothers, enslavement in Egypt, and wrongful imprisonment, Joseph rose to prominence through his God-given ability to interpret dreams. His gifts not only elevated him to a position of authority but ultimately served as a means to save not only his family but an entire nation from famine. From the depths of despair, Joseph's journey showcases the transformative power of using one's gifts to serve and protect others.

Similarly, King David, renowned for his leadership and musical talents, began as a humble shepherd boy. His journey to becoming a king was marked by his ability to rally others and inspire courage in the face of adversities. David's story illustrates that a significant impact often begins in seemingly mundane circumstances. For firstborns, this is a reminder that influence doesn't require grand stages; even acts of kindness and service in one's immediate environment can spark profound changes.

Firstborns are often inherently perceived as caregivers, naturally stepping into roles of support and encouragement. These attributes can be leveraged to build healthier family dynamics, promote unity in communities, and inspire change in societal structures. Whether it's through mentoring younger siblings, volunteering in local community services, or leading initiatives that address social issues, firstborns possess a unique opportunity to shape their surroundings positively.

Recognizing the various gifts that firstborns can offer is essential. Some may possess extraordinary organizational skills that can facilitate community events, whereas others may be naturally inclined to engage with younger generations in mentoring roles. The relational aptitude many firstborns exhibit enables them to connect with others in ways that foster understanding and cooperation. Whether it's emotional intelligence, creativity in problem-solving, or the capacity to inspire with words, these gifts hold immense potential.

To make a tangible impact, firstborns must actively pursue opportunities to serve. Volunteering at local charities, being involved in church activities, or organizing community clean-up projects are practical ways firstborns can step up. Serving within one's community not only fulfills personal growth but also aligns with the Christian call to love and serve others. It echoes Jesus' teachings, emphasizing that greatness comes from serving rather than being served.

Moreover, firstborns bear the unique position of being seen as role models. This inherently holds a responsibility to model positive behavior and attitudes. There is so much power in being an example of hope, perseverance, and faith. For instance, a firstborn who navigates the complexities of life with grace can significantly influence their peers' and siblings' choices. They carry the baton of influence, which they can use to guide others toward constructive paths.

In the workplace, firstborns can also make substantial contributions. Whether it be leading teams, inspiring innovators, or serving as catalysts for change, their roles can build strong foundations that motivate and empower others. Possessing an acute sense of responsibility often drives firstborns to exceed expectations. This ambition can be harnessed to improve workplace culture, foster collaboration, and ingrain uplifting values. A firstborn leader who prioritizes empathy while championing the collective goals can turn work environments into thriving spaces of productivity and positivity.

Education is another arena where firstborns can leave lasting impressions. They can tutor younger students, assist peers in study groups, or advocate for educational reforms to ensure that all students receive a fair chance to learn and grow. Being aware of the challenges faced by others allows firstborns to step into educator roles, sharing knowledge and experiences that pave the way for others.

Mentorship is a gift that firstborns can embrace with passion. By actively investing in younger siblings or peers, firstborns can provide guidance and encouragement, sometimes steering them away from pitfalls they have encountered. As they share their insights, they foster a sense of belonging and confidence in their mentees, which can create a ripple effect across communities.

Communicating with authentic compassion is crucial for firstborns looking to impact others. In a world that can often feel harsh and critical, bringing kindness and understanding to interactions elevates the importance of empathy. Firstborns can create safe spaces where others feel seen, heard, and valued. By extending grace to others, they strengthen connections and encourage collective healing and growth.

Firstborns can also utilize technology to amplify their impact. With platforms like social media, blogs, and podcasts, they are provided tools to share their messages and experiences broadly. This enables them to reach a wider audience, fostering connections that transcend geographical boundaries. By sharing empowering content or highlighting community endeavors, they can inspire others to take action in their own lives.

However, firstborns need to remember that they, too, need support on their journey to positively impacting the world. Building strong support systems can help them navigate the challenges they face. Community, whether it originates from family, friends, or colleagues, becomes a vital source of emotional and spiritual nourishment that allows firstborns to rejuvenate and refocus their energies on service. Navigating expectations can be daunting for firstborns, especially when pressure mounts. Therefore, creating space for self-care and spiritual renewal is crucial. Engaging in prayer, meditation, and community worship enables firstborns to ground themselves in their purpose and realign their path to one that reflects God's love. Community service initiatives are powerful entry points for firstborns to engage actively with their localities. Participating in initiatives like food drives, youth programs, or environmental conservation efforts not only enriches their communities but also fosters interpersonal connections that strengthen the fabric of society. By understanding the needs of their communities, firstborns can cultivate empathy and awareness that positions them for greater impact.

The arts can also be a compelling avenue for firstborns to express their gifts. Whether through music, painting, writing, or performance, arts serve as a language that can bridge gaps between people. Firstborns can use their creative platforms to tell stories that highlight social issues, promote positive messages, or bring joy to those around them. By engaging others through artistic expressions, they can deliver impactful narratives that stir emotions and inspire action.

Youth programs are particularly important avenues for firstborns to nurture emerging leaders. Organized events that bring youths together around shared interests or community challenges can foster leadership qualities in both firstborns and their peers. By facilitating workshops, mentorship sessions, or team-building activities, firstborns can instill values of teamwork and integrity while providing support for their growth.

Eventually, engaging in advocacy is another way firstborns can impact the world positively. Whether through raising awareness about social justice, environmental issues, or mental health, firstborns can utilize their voices and positions to influence change. Firstborns equipped with knowledge about the issues they are passionate about can advocate effectively, mobilizing communities to support essential causes.

As firstborns consider their pathways to making a difference, they need to embrace a mindset of gratitude. Recognizing the blessings they have received equips them with the perspective needed to serve others genuinely. This grateful heart positions them to act selflessly and cultivate environments of positivity. As they engage in service, they can reflect on the countless ways they have been blessed, which further fuels their desire to extend those blessings to others.

To culminate this subchapter, I challenge firstborns to take concrete steps toward making a sustained impact in their communities and beyond. Start with small actions—extend a helping hand to a neighbor in need, volunteer at a local charity, or launch a community-driven initiative that aligns with your passion. No matter how insignificant a gesture may seem, it can create rippling effects of change that elevate lives and bring communities together.

Consider setting specific goals that encourage you to donate your time or resources. Whether it's dedicating one day a month to volunteerism or mentoring a young person, cultivate a habit of active participation. Measure progress, celebrate victories, and allow those experiences to empower you to push further into your calling.

Don't forget to invite others on this journey—create partnerships or collaborations that align desires and strengths toward a common goal. Together, identify shared interests that drive collective action, resulting in more considerable influence and impact.

As firstborns fulfill their divine purposes, they can redirect their energies to uplift and support those around them. The responsibility that accompanies being a firstborn should not be viewed as a burden but rather as an opportunity to create positive change in the world. With every motivated action, they can honor God and uplift humanity, becoming beacons of hope amid darkness.

In the tapestry of life, firstborns have the potential to weave narratives of resilience and impact that resonate through generations. By recognizing the power of their gifts, committing to serve, and encouraging others, they can be catalysts for transformation, grounded in faith and empowered by love. Standing united in purpose, firstborns can leave indelible marks on the world, inspiring communities to become brighter and more hopeful places to live. Together, they can rise to fulfill their calling and embrace their roles as agents of change.

CHAPTER 30

A VISION FOR THE FUTURE

As we conclude this journey together, it is with a heart full of hope and a mind ignited by the possibilities that lie ahead for firstborns. The narrative of the firstborn, woven through the fabric of cultures, families, and scriptures, is one rich in complexity and depth. It is a story that encompasses not only trials and tribulations but also triumphs and transformations. This subchapter serves as a clarion call, inviting each of you to envision a future marked by empowerment, identity, and an unwavering sense of purpose.

Throughout this book, we have explored the weight that comes with being a firstborn. We have delved into the cultural significance, the psychological pressures, and the spiritual battles faced by those who occupy this vital role within families and communities. Yet, in acknowledging these challenges, we have consistently pointed to the light of hope found in Jesus Christ, the ultimate firstborn. His life, death, and resurrection serve as the cornerstone of our faith, demonstrating that despite the difficulties we may encounter, there is redemption and restoration available to all.

Reflecting on the themes of identity, we are reminded that being a firstborn is not simply about the burdens we carry or the expectations placed upon us. It is about recognizing who we are in Christ. Our identities are not shaped by societal norms or family expectations but by our relationship with our Creator. In Him, we are seen as heirs, worthy and valued. This identity is not a passive one; it is an active force that propels us toward our God-given destinies.

As firstborns, we are called to be leaders and trailblazers. This calling may manifest in various ways—through acts of service in our communities, mentorship roles within our families, or by passionately pursuing our creative ambitions. Every firstborn has within them the potential to impact lives positively, to inspire change, and to carry forth the legacy of faith that has been entrusted to us.

Many firstborns shoulder the expectation of perfectionism and achievement, often leading them to an internal struggle. However, the beauty of the gospel is that it frees us from the bonds of performance-based identity. Our worth is not contingent on our accomplishments but on the unconditional love of Christ. This realization allows us to step boldly into the future, unencumbered by the fears of inadequacy or failure. Remember that the journey of faith is about progress and not perfection. We are encouraged to learn, grow, and transform continuously.

In embracing a victorious mindset, we must also clarify our vision for the future. What does it look like to live as empowered firstborns fully aware of our identities in Christ? It means adopting a lens of optimism, even when circumstances appear bleak. It involves engaging in communities that support and uplift us, fostering connections that draw out our strengths and encourage our spiritual growth. Firstborns have a unique opportunity to build bridges, cultivate relationships, and foster environments where others can thrive.

The notion of community is paramount to this vision. As we reflect on the critical role of firstborns within family and society, we recognize that we do not walk this path alone. We are part of a broader community of believers, a family of faith that stands united in purpose. When we lean on one another, share our burdens, and celebrate our victories, we embody the spirit of Christ—a spirit that encourages us to bear each other's loads and forge ahead together. Imagine a future where firstborns take their rightful place as leaders in their families and communities. Visualize them stepping confidently into roles of influence, whether in their workplaces, schools, or churches. Picture them advocating for the marginalized, mentoring younger generations, and standing as pillars of hope and strength in their communities. This vision is achievable, but it requires action on our part.

As we envision this future, we must not underestimate the power of our commitments and actions. It is time to recommit ourselves to the journey of faith—one that is characterized by growth, humility, and a willingness to learn. Each day is an opportunity to make choices aligned with our values, to pray for guidance, and to seek wisdom from God. By pursuing a life of integrity and faithfulness, we create ripples of influence that extend far beyond our immediate surroundings.

Moreover, a commitment to personal growth is essential. We need to cultivate a learning attitude, wherein we actively seek to deepen our understanding of God and our purpose. This involves engaging in scripture study, embracing mentorship opportunities, and surrounding ourselves with people who challenge and inspire us. As we invest time in our spiritual development, we refine our understanding of what it means to be a firstborn in the Kingdom of God.

As you move forward, I encourage you to carry the message of victory and empowerment into your lives and communities. Share the lessons learned throughout this book with others; be vulnerable and open about your journey with firstborn status, and how faith has transformed those struggles. Your stories will resonate with many who find themselves lost or burdened by their roles. By sharing your triumphs and tribulations, you offer hope to others walking similar paths.

In this vision for the future, we affirm that transformation is not limited to individual experiences. As we live out our identities as firstborns, we have the profound ability to impact our families and communities positively. We become agents of change, encouraging family members to embrace their unique identities and to heal from generational patterns that may hinder their growth. By doing so, we not only break generational curses but also establish a legacy of faith, resilience, and empowerment for the next generation.

As we look ahead, let us seize the opportunities before us with optimism and courage. The future is not something to fear but a canvas on which we can paint our stories of growth and purpose. Consider setting goals that align with your calling as a firstborn, whether in your personal, academic, or professional life. Ask yourself what specific steps you can take to make a positive difference in your community, and embark on that journey with intention.

Moreover, remember that it is okay to seek assistance along the way. Acknowledging our challenges and seeking help is not a sign of weakness but a testament to our commitment to growth. Engaging in supportive communities, reaching out to mentors, or even seeking professional guidance can provide the necessary tools for navigating the complexities of life as a firstborn. Remember that your journey is an ongoing process, and each step forward is progress in itself.

Finally, let us create a culture of celebration and encouragement. A future filled with hope and empowerment is cultivated not only through individual efforts but also through collective support. Celebrate the victories of others; uplift their strengths and assist them in overcoming their challenges. By fostering a community of encouragement, we reinforce the belief that we are all in this journey together and that every story matters.

In conclusion, the vision for the future of firstborns is one of hope, empowerment, and community engagement. As you embark on this journey, may you embrace your identity as a child of God, fully realizing your potential and purpose. Understand that you are not defined by your struggles; instead, you are shaped by the grace of God that enables you to rise above them.

Together, let us commit ourselves to fostering communities rooted in faith, hope, and love. Let us embrace our roles as firstborns with enthusiasm, recognizing that the battles fought and the victories won shape not only our lives but also the narrative of those who come after us. May we move forward with confidence, equipped for the journey ahead, and ready to create a legacy of faith that impacts generations to come.

Your story is still being written, and the pages ahead are blank, teeming with the potential for growth and transformation. Step boldly into your identity, carry forth the message of victory, and let us make the future as firstborns a beautiful testament to the grace and power of God in our lives. Your time to shine and make a difference is now. Embrace it!

TO MY WONDERFUL READERS.

Thank you, lovely readers, for embarking on this journey with me! This book is more than just a collection of insights; it's a heartfelt exploration that has the potential to ignite your spirit and reshape your understanding of what it means to be a firstborn. I know we've shared many layers of wisdom, struggles, and victories as we navigated through the unique tapestry of spiritual warfare that accompanies this role. I want you to stand proud in that identity and yield your strengths to help shape the world around you.

As you close this book now—or perhaps take a moment to linger on the last words—I hope you carry with you an uplifting spirit and a renewed sense of purpose. You are not alone! The stories we've embraced together, filled with faith and transformation, are testaments to the incredible resilience within each of you. Your struggles are valid, but your victories? They're groundbreaking! These triumphs deserve to be shared loud and clear to inspire others who may have walked a similar path.

The essence of our journey has been the understanding that we possess the power to break generational curses and not be ensnared by negativity. Instead, let us forge ahead hand in hand with joy, embracing the beautiful identity God has crafted just for us. In doing so, you can continually claim your victory, step into your calling, and nurture the support of your community.

Take heart in knowing that your lived experiences have equipped you with the tools to contribute positively to the world, to your families, and even to your communities. This is your moment! Let every triumph you've read about in this book resonate within you, fueling your passion to make a difference. The world is waiting for your voice, for your leadership. It's time to step into it!

As we part, I want to encourage you to keep the spirit flowing. Continue exploring these themes, share your stories with others, and let's keep the conversations alive. Anyway, all of this together has reminded us how profoundly connected we are as firstborns! Each love-filled hug shared, each whispered encouragement passed on, gives life to our missions and fortifies our spirit. Thank you for joining me on this incredible adventure. Now go forth, claim your legacy, and embrace the ride ahead with faith and an unstoppable mindset.

With infinite love and solidarity,

Forever cheering for you
Prof. Michael T. Adenitire, FBI; PH.D.

AKNOWLEDGEMENTS

My profound gratitude goes to the Almighty GOD: the FATHER, the SON, and the HOLY SPIRIT, for His grace to put this book together.

I acknowledge the students at Zoe Pentecostal Bible Institute & Seminary, both past and present, for your contribution in the classroom as we studied together some sections of the book.

I acknowledge all the members of Zoe Pentecostal Mission, where I have preached most of the messages in this book.

To my late Mother, Madam Victoria Adenitire, though you have gone to rest with the LORD, your investment in my education has made this book possible.

I thank my daughter, Mrs. Ruth Olutosin Badmus, and my son, Mr. Emmanuel Olukayode Adenitire, who both formed a team with me to find the best publisher for the book and offered constructive suggestions to make the best book in the market. I am grateful.

I cannot forget my wife, Dr. Mabel Olufunmilayo Adenitire, who created the enabling environment for this book. I deeply appreciate you, darling.

DEDICATION.

I dedicate this book to biological and providential firstborns. Be assured that victory is yours as you go through the battles of life and you rely on the grace of God.

www.ingramcontent.com/pod-product-compliance
Lightning Source LLC
Chambersburg PA
CBHW021106130626
46554CB00002B/556